Unleash Your Meeting Potential™

A Comprehensive Guide to Leading Effective Meetings

1st Edition

NATALIE BERKIW, PMP

Published by Natalie Berkiw, PMP
Royal Oak, Michigan, USA

ISBN: 978-0-9996187-1-4 (Hardcover)
ISBN: 978-0-9996187-0-7 (Paperback)

Library of Congress Control Number: 2017918291

1st Edition – 2017

Share this book with your team – and save!
Unleash Your Meeting Potential™ is filled with valuable information for leaders and staff members at every level. Bulk order discounts are available to corporations, associations, and others, when you order multiple copies to distribute to teams or for use in corporate training programs. For more information, contact the publisher directly about sales of books in quantities of 75+, at:

Natalie Berkiw, PMP
natalieberkiw@gmail.com
www.EffectiveMeetings101.com

Dedication

This book is dedicated to all the inspiring people I have had the pleasure of participating in meetings with. To the many people over the years who have come to me for guidance and coaching on leading more effective meetings, you were the inspiration and catalyst for this work.

I especially want to thank my wonderful, supportive fiancé Adam, for his patience and motivation, while I spent countless hours writing, editing and formatting this book over the past two years.

About the Author

Natalie Berkiw has been successfully leading effective meetings as a seasoned, senior project management consultant, for the past 17 years. She holds a Project Management Professional (PMP) designation through the global Project Management Institute, and certification in Lean from the University of Michigan's College of Engineering.

Natalie has international experience leading meetings in both Canada and the United States. She has worked primarily in the health care and non-profit sectors and has extensive experience in team and meeting facilitation, strategic planning, project management and process improvement. With her years of experience participating in meetings daily with CEOs, executive teams, managers and frontline staff, she has translated her learning into *The 3 Step Meeting Framework*™.

She currently lives in Royal Oak, Michigan with her fiancé Adam, and their dog Sasha.

Table of Contents

Chapter 1

Introduction to Unleash Your Meeting Potential™

How often do you *wait in anticipation* for a meeting in your calendar? How often have you left a meeting feeling a *sense of satisfaction* and accomplishment?

Perhaps your answers to both questions are "not often" or possibly "never at all." But, why?

Evidence suggests **we universally love to *hate* meetings**. They're one of the few, shared experiences that provide us with a tremendous source of *anxiety, boredom, and stress*. This shared dislike is a result of attending countless, poorly planned and executed meetings. The fact you're exploring this book tells me that you're frustrated and had enough with the status quo.

Meetings are one of the *most common business activities* across nearly every industry, and yet, they continue to be one of the top complaints by leadership and staff alike. They take place at every level from the executive teams to front-line staff. Billions of dollars are invested into meetings by organizations globally every year. Consider the number of people, salaries, time, resources and overhead costs that are spent on meetings, and you will quickly see how these costs can escalate.

Research has shown that the same frustrations are expressed by meeting participants everywhere. See if these *common experiences* listed below are familiar to you:

BEFORE THE MEETING

❑ The **purpose** of the meeting isn't clear
❑ A lack of **information** is pre-circulated
❑ **No agenda** is developed
❑ The **logistics** are unclear (Where is that meeting room?)
❑ **No expectations** are set around how participants should prepare in advance

DURING THE MEETING

❑ The meeting **starts late**
❑ People show up **wondering** what the meeting is about
❑ No one knows **why they were invited**
❑ Too much time is spent **giving updates**
❑ Some participants **dominate** the discussion
❑ **Decisions** can't be reached and are constantly put off
❑ The lead doesn't seem to be **leading** the meeting
❑ Conversations frequently run **off-track** and are not brought back
❑ It feels **unsafe** to voice an opinion or feels like input **isn't valued**
❑ People who should contribute **don't speak up**
❑ The meeting ends **without any next steps** identified
❑ No one **documents** the discussion, so it's lost after the meeting
❑ The meeting **ends late**

AFTER THE MEETING

❑ No one is clear about their **responsibilities**
❑ There is **lack of follow through** on identified action items
❑ There is **no communication** after the meeting

Did your top frustrations make the list? Can you think of a few more? Indeed, there are many.

Now that we have a sense of some classic meeting concerns, let's steer this conversation in another direction.

What is a meeting?
A meeting can be defined as a *gathering of two or more people to discuss specific topics, risks, issues, and to make decisions, for a specific duration of time.*

Sadly, a large portion of meetings are ineffectively planned, executed and followed up on. As a result, it's been demonstrated that there are *substantial emotional and cultural costs* associated with frequent, ineffective meetings.

A few of these costs include the following:

• Participants feel like their **time isn't valued**
• Teams experience **meeting fatigue**
• **Time is taken away** from other important activities
• Projects and **initiatives stall** and don't move forward
• Communications and **relationships break down**
• **Staff morale** is impacted
• Organizational goals are **not achieved**
• Time and money are **wasted** through a loss of productivity
• The workplace culture of the organization **slowly deteriorates**
• Unhappy staff lead to **greater turnover**

Wait, all the above can result from ineffective meetings? Yes! Meetings can be a large, contributing factor to the issues outlined above. So many organizations live this reality every day. In fact, many never even realize it. Even if they do recognize there is an issue, they don't have the slightest idea on how to fix it, or where to get the support to do so.

Meetings are a standard business activity that organizations expect from their leadership and staff. However, solid principles around meeting management are *never taught in school*. Further to this, most organizations *fail to offer training*. So, where are these skills learned?

What would an ideal future state look like?
All of us go to work wanting to do our best and to feel like we make a difference. If meetings are part of your day, then an ideal, future state might look like this:

• Meetings are productive and **add value**
• Something important is **accomplished** in every meeting
• Everyone knows what is expected of them and has **clarity** in their roles and responsibilities
• There is **collaboration** between teams
• Everyone feels valued for their input and **feels heard**
• **Strong relationships** are built based on good communication and trust
• Projects and initiatives **move forward** successfully

What if meetings were always planned, executed and followed up on *effectively and consistently*? Over a short time, this list could easily be achieved.

But, what would it take to make this happen? The first and critical step in achieving this optimal state is exploring the opportunity for *appropriate standardization* in how meetings are approached.

What is appropriate standardization?

Every meeting is unique. The purpose, objectives, participants, logistics, agenda, etc. are all meeting-specific. Many elements are and should continue to be, customizable.

However, where there are opportunities for improvements are in the *steps and activities before, during and after a meeting*. It is here where standardization could add true benefit and value to leaders, staff, and organizations everywhere. Part of the answer is around *completing the appropriate steps in the right sequence*. The rest of the answer is doing them *consistently*.

Imagine if all meeting leads were trained with a simple, straight-forward and replicable methodology around effective meeting management.

By refining the skills of leaders and staff, and enabling them to consistently lead more effective meetings, then the following results are possible:

• Organizations are more **productive and profitable**
• People feel more **valued and respected**
• Workplace culture and staff morale **thrive**

What will you learn in this book?

Consider this as a guide that offers foundational knowledge about leading effective business meetings. This book aims to address the substantial gap between our current state and the ideal future state by providing you with a practical framework and methodology. This will allow you to close the gap between the meeting challenges of today and the future success of tomorrow.

In the next chapter, I will introduce ***The 3 Step Meeting Framework™*** that will guide you through each of the activities you should follow *before, during* and *after* a meeting. As you read this book, my goals for you are to:

- Learn each of the **standardized steps and activities**
- Identify what you are **already doing well** and where you could **make improvements** to your own current state
- Explore how you can **apply these simple activities** and immediately improve how you and your organization approach and lead meetings

While this book describes each step in considerable detail, the application of the methodology is *easy*. It applies common sense to meeting management.

Figure 1.1: Learning, Applying and Mastering The 3 Step Meeting Framework™

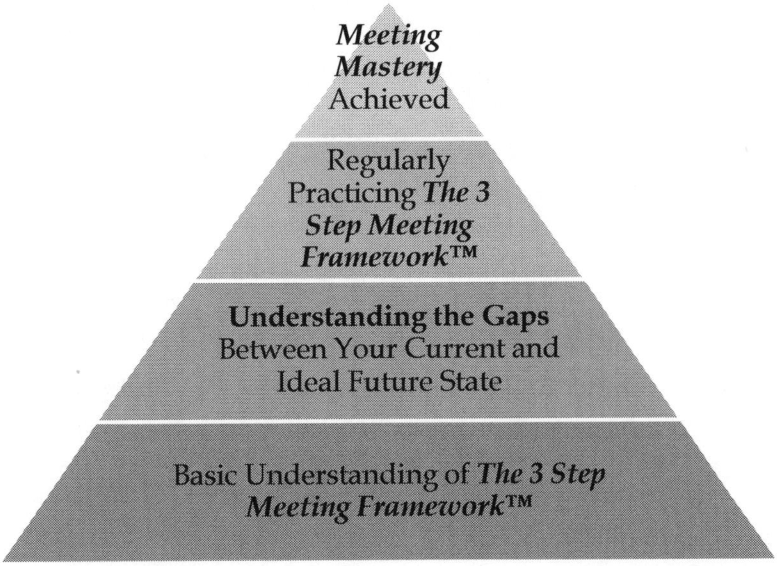
Meeting Mastery Achieved
Regularly Practicing The 3 Step Meeting Framework™
Understanding the Gaps Between Your Current and Ideal Future State
Basic Understanding of The 3 Step Meeting Framework™

Each reader comes from a different perspective, industry, and background. This means that your personal experience reading this book and what you take away from it will also be slightly different.

You may find you're already doing some of these activities in the methodology. If so, good for you! Look for opportunities to implement the remaining steps and activities to maximize the effectiveness and productivity of your meetings. Read through each activity and pick up the steps or considerations that you have perhaps overlooked, have not paid enough attention to, or can simply enhance.

Remember, *culture change takes time and effort*. But, improving one meeting at a time will support the needed changes and add value to all participants involved.

What will you not find here?

There are many resources, books, websites, blogs, etc. that are dedicated to meeting management. Some of them are *dotted* with wise advice and valuable suggestions. However, far too many offer impractical suggestions, and others are simply inappropriate for most business settings.

I want to be clear about what you will *not* find in this book to set any expectations upfront.

- **Parliamentary rules of order** – While a few concepts overlap, parliamentary rules are not reviewed or discussed in this book. These meeting rules are built on older principles and only have applications in a few, select meeting environments, such as some board committee meetings. I have found these rules are an inappropriate fit with the culture of most business environments today. However, if this suits your needs, there are many valuable resources available to you.

- **Gimmicky acronyms or silly suggestions** – There seems to be a wide variety of ideas out there around improving meetings. These continue to provide a false sense of hope and offer unsustainable results. If you need to learn a new terminology or set of tools with *made-up* acronyms instead of using common sense, don't waste your time. These are not sustainable, and you will forget these acronyms within a few days.

I will not suggest you hold "stand-up only" meetings and tell you to take away the chairs. As a woman who often wears heels, I beg you, please never do this. This approach would not work in most work environments. I'm sure anyone with chronic back pain would also agree.

Food should never be suggested as a mandatory for meetings to be successful. Those offering this idea have not taken into consideration that many businesses, especially non-profits, do not have operational budgets for this.

This also includes offering participants promotional items like squeeze balls and fancy pens. People may be temporarily amused, but these unnecessary additions will not set the meeting up for success.

Another entertaining suggestion you will not find here is the idea of removing meetings all together. This is unrealistic, doesn't address the underlying issues, and fails to offer a practical solution.

Who will benefit from this book?
Unleash Your Meeting Potential™ is beneficial for new, aspiring and seasoned leaders and managers, consultants, project managers, and students preparing for the business environment. This book is also a valuable resource for organizational development consultants and talent management teams who support staff and professional training and development.

About the author - Who am I?
Before we start to delve into this book further, let me introduce myself. My name is Natalie Berkiw. Like many of you, I lead and participate in multiple meetings every day. As a senior project management consultant, meetings are a large part of my life. I can honestly say I've never had a day when I haven't taken away a key lesson learned from these experiences.

I have had the privilege of sitting with CEOs, executive teams, leaders, and front-line staff to support strategic planning and to lead various projects and initiatives. Early in my career, I sought to emulate the most influential leaders in my organizations. But I found that great learning opportunities also came from others that were far less experienced. I have trialed and errored along the way and benefitted greatly from the learning these experiences afforded me.

Over time, I *began to see patterns in the meetings* that were successful and those that never achieved any outcomes. Along with my years of observations and stories shared by others, I started to identify the key steps and activities that, when done well, **produced great results**. I quickly excelled in my career at an early age and was constantly requested by leaders in my organization to drive their strategic initiatives forward.

I became passionate about helping others reach the success that I was achieving and began sharing my learning with others. Coaching and mentoring those around me to succeed became a motivator for me. I quickly realized that I could have a broader impact beyond my inner circles. I became inspired to share my success with the world with the goal of making meetings more effective everywhere. From here, I launched an educational website called **EffectiveMeetings101.com** and started on the adventure of writing this book that you hold in your hands today.

Meetings can be a *powerful enabler in achieving success in your career*. Use this book as a step-by-step guide to leading meetings that are worth having. Instead of a shared dislike for meetings, my goal is to help you achieve a *shared respect and appreciation* of the value meetings can offer you. I hope to also eliminate the resulting stress, anxiety, and boredom along the way.

Chapter 2

The 3 Step Meeting Framework™

As a project management professional and consultant, I have spent hours every day for years in nearly every kind of meeting imaginable. After seeing countless meetings achieve successful results and numerous others fall flat, I began to quickly see what was done before, during and after these meetings that contributed to each of their successes or failures.

Through some trial and error, I began to test out these patterns and found that by following several key activities, in the appropriate sequence, *I could achieve the results I wanted consistently.*

> *Using this knowledge, I began to develop a simple, replicable framework that could be easily followed by anyone. This became the basis of how I developed **The 3 Step Meeting Framework™**.*

In this chapter, I lay out **The 3 Step Meeting Framework™** along with the methodology you can follow for each step. This straightforward, common sense approach is applicable in nearly every industry and environment. Use this book to guide you through the activities you haven't thought of, are not doing well, or use this as an opportunity to build on your existing knowledge and skills.

What are the steps in *The 3 Step Meeting Framework™*?

The framework contains the three, logical steps to any meeting. They are outlined below.

Figure 2.1: The 3 Step Meeting Framework™

Surely, this *sounds* far too simple. However, I have found in my years of experience that critical tasks and activities within one or more of these steps are missed or poorly executed. This results in meetings that are unproductive, lack any tangible outcomes, and are a waste of time for the participants and the organization.

To get at the heart of *The 3 Step Meeting Framework™*, let's walk through the steps and the activities outlined for each. The details of the activities are explained further in the chapters that follow.

Step 1: BEFORE the Meeting

The planning required is often underestimated but is essential to achieving a successful meeting. Here are the sequenced activities for *Step 1: Before the Meeting*:

1.	Define your **meeting purpose**.
2.	Determine your meeting **objectives and expected outcomes**.
3.	Identify the right **people** to invite.
4.	Determine the right **format** for your meeting.
5.	Identify the **logistics** for the meeting.
6.	Develop and circulate a **meeting appointment**.

| 7. Develop a clear, sequenced **agenda**. |
| 8. Determine the **room layout** for your meeting. |
| 9. Determine the **resources and tools** you need. |
| 10. Develop and circulate a **meeting communication and package**. |

Step 2: DURING the Meeting

This step consists of the actual meeting itself and includes everything from set-up to take-down. Here are the sequenced activities for *Step 2: During the Meeting*:

| 11. **Set up** before the meeting. |
| 12. **Welcome** the participants and capture **attendance**. |
| 13. **Review the agenda** and **lay out expectations**. |
| 14. Provide **high-level context-setting** including the purpose, objectives and expected outcomes. |
| 15. **Lead** the meeting discussion. |
| 16. **Capture and document** the meeting discussion. |
| 17. Review the **action items** and define the **next steps**. |
| 18. Set any **post-meeting expectations**. |
| 19. **Evaluate the meeting** and capture any **lessons learned**. |
| 20. **Thank** the participants and **close** the meeting. |

Step 3: AFTER the Meeting

Following up after a meeting is often skipped over. This leaves all the great work done to fall short and fail to cross the finish line. Just because the meeting has ended, doesn't mean your efforts stop there. Here are the sequenced activities for *Step 3: After the Meeting*:

| 21. Collect **all meeting notes** and develop **meeting minutes** or an **action log**. |
| 22. Develop and circulate a **follow-up meeting communication and package**. |
| 23. **Evaluate** the meeting outcomes and process. |

24. Follow up on all **action items**.
25. Plan any required **follow-up meetings** and apply **lessons learned** to future meetings.

The three steps outlined above along with the 25 sequenced activities make up the framework and methodology of *The 3 Step Meeting Framework™*.

You will learn more as you begin to explore the chapters in this book. Expect to find the activities of each step defined in detail along with a variety of examples to better illustrate the information.

To enhance your learning and put these steps into practice, look for and follow along with the **Unleash Your Meeting Potential™ Workbook**, sold separately. This workbook will walk you through the steps and activities with exercises, templates, and detailed instructions. The **Unleash Your Meeting Potential™ 16"x 20" Wall Poster**, also available, will allow you to maintain a visual reminder of the framework in your office, boardroom, lunchroom, etc.

Let's begin to delve further into each step and activity of the framework.

Step 1: *Before* the Meeting

Step 1	Step 2	Step 3
Before	*During*	*After*

Define the Meeting Purpose

Have you ever sat in a meeting wondering why the group was pulled together? If so, you're not alone. Unfortunately, far too many meetings are organized without completing the *first, foundational step of planning.* Before pulling participants together, the *reason* for doing so should be clearly identified. Determining the purpose answers the important question of *why* you need a meeting.

There are many valid reasons to bring people together. This chapter highlights the *most common reasons* to hold a meeting and describes the importance of each.

Meetings must have *at least* one identified purpose. However, if you find you can't answer the fundamental question of why you need a meeting, then think twice about having one.

What are the common reasons to have a meeting?

The purpose of your meeting should be *directly tied to your specific business activities* and is likely to fall within one or more of these categories:

• Brainstorming
• Decision-making
• Educating
• Gaining buy-in
• Identifying and assessing needs
• Information-sharing

• Planning
• Prioritizing
• Problem-solving
• Promoting, selling or offering a new solution
• Working

Each of these meeting purposes are described in further detail below.

Brainstorming

Brainstorming is *all about idea generation*. These meetings are focused around a defined scope or topic that is understood by everyone in the room. *Ideas are discussed openly* and captured for consideration. The discussion could be very specific, such as identifying activities and tasks required for a project, or as broad as all the possible initiatives an organization might want to do over the coming year to meet its strategic objectives.

Brainstorming meetings are a great opportunity to *bring multiple perspectives to the table* for a "one-time only" commitment. This allows you to gain their input early on instead of after an idea or initiative is fully planned. This avoids the need to backtrack later because a key perspective was missed.

Instead of taking days, weeks or months to gather various perspectives individually, this can be done with great success in only a few hours together during a brainstorming meeting.

Decision-making

Meetings are often pulled together for the purpose of *making a decision*. This could be strategic or operational in nature. Depending on the unique needs of each required decision, the *key decision-makers will be different*. The level of authority will depend on the situation. Some decisions will be made by one person, either with or without input from others. Others will be made collectively as a group.

These meetings begin with context-setting and outlining the decision needed. This is followed by a review or brainstorming of the options. The discussion provides the decision-makers with the information needed to *make an informed decision* on how to move forward appropriately.

These meetings *allow organizations to move forward* when key decisions are required. Examples include high-level, strategic decisions such as what area of their business they want to focus on going forward, or detailed, operational decisions around processes and daily practices.

Projects or initiatives also require frequent decisions. As a new idea or opportunity is explored, planned, implemented and closed out, there are times when key decisions are needed during the project team and steering committee meetings.

Educating

Some meetings are pulled together *to educate the participants*. Many industries and positions require:

• Initial training upon hiring
• Maintaining education credits for a professional designation
• Skills to be maintained or upgraded
• Personal and professional development

Some education is *mandatory* for leaders and staff, while other opportunities are *optional* and out of interest. These meetings are scheduled for a single session or completed over multiple sessions for a specific duration of time.

Education meetings offer *great opportunities for team-building* since participants can support each other during the learning and then leave with a shared, common understanding of the educational content.

Just-in-time training is another valuable reason to hold an education meeting. This provides the participants with new knowledge and skills right before they are required to take on new responsibilities or being exposed to changes. This could be related to changes in their job description, new processes and protocols, the workplace environment, etc.

Education meetings can benefit the participants and the organization by:

• Maintaining quality and safety standards
• Growing the knowledge level and skill sets within leaders and staff
• Providing an environment where continuing education and skill enhancement is valued

Gaining buy-in

Meetings to gain buy-in are *to walk people through an upcoming change and to gain their support and acceptance.* Buy-in meetings allow you to openly discuss possible future changes with your participants who need to understand what is changing, the potential impacts, and how they can support the changes. A few examples of changes that might require buy-in include:

• Processes and workflows
• Policies and procedures
• Staffing requirements
• Physical environment
• New projects or initiatives
• Additional funding

This type of meeting is a step beyond an information-sharing meeting as some level of *engagement, support and endorsement* are needed. Participants have the potential to *positively or negatively impact the implementation* of the changes. Go into these meetings knowing what level of support you require from them so you can engage them appropriately.

Gaining buy-in

Identifying and assessing needs

A meeting to identify and assess needs is to *understand what issues, challenges, gaps or requirements exist to support the development of an appropriate solution or response.* Meet with leaders, clients, sponsors or other key individuals to determine their specific needs and to set expectations.

These meetings allow for information gathering with the right perspectives around the table. This provides you with an opportunity to collect and share essential information that leads to the *development of the right solution* to meet any unique and specific needs.

Identifying needs

Information-sharing

An information-sharing meeting offers an opportunity to inform participants regarding any updates or upcoming changes. These could include the following:

• New policies and procedures
• The implementation of a new workflow process
• The kick-off or go-live of a new project, program or initiative
• Any other upcoming changes

These meetings are held to provide information that is *too complex to describe through other means* including email or social media and/or has the possibility of *evoking an emotional response*. Information is presented to the group with an opportunity for questions, clarity and level setting.

Meetings to share information are valuable as they provide your participants with timely content that is aligned with a planned, upcoming change. This allows the *same key messaging* to be shared with everyone at one time.

Information-sharing

Planning

Planning meetings bring participants together to *plan the details of a project, program, process, product, service or workplan.* These meetings provide an opportunity to bring various perspectives and expertise to the table to provide input into a planning process.

These meetings occur at both the *corporate, strategic level* through to the *detailed, operational level.* All organizations complete some level of strategic planning that pulls together various people and inputs to determine the organization's direction. With this direction set, it allows the operational teams to plan the details to operationalize the strategic plan.

Projects and initiatives require planning teams and committees. These groups come together to:

• Define the scope of a project or initiative
• Identify the required activities
• Sequence the activities and develop a schedule
• Define the resource requirements
• Identify and manage the risks and issues
• Support the details of implementation

Bring your participants together for a planning meeting to collaboratively define and implement a plan to move a project, initiative or goal forward.

Prioritizing

Meetings with the purpose of prioritization are meant to *prioritize strategies, initiatives or activities of an organization, team or project.* Participants will review these items through the lens of what should move forward in the short-term, long-term or perhaps, not at all.

Prioritizing explores what activities provide the *greatest impact or return on investment (ROI) versus the level of effort and resources required* to move them forward. However, the criteria for prioritizing is unique to your situation.

All organizations identify numerous activities and initiatives that could add value. However, unless resources are infinite, it's highly unlikely that everything can move forward at the same time. Prioritizing meetings evaluate all the options and determine where resources and efforts should be placed.

Problem-solving

Some meetings are intended for problem-solving where the *participants work through the complexities of a problem, issue or risk with the goals of overcoming the challenge and defining next steps.*

Organizations face new challenges on an ongoing basis. While some of these problems are minor, others could have significant impacts. Expertise is needed to come together to work through these issues as they arise. These meetings allow organizations to be *flexible and nimble, and address challenges quickly.*

Promoting, selling or offering a new solution

Solution-based meetings occur when *a new idea, product, service or project is presented as a solution to address an identified gap or need.* After a needs assessment is complete, a response to those needs is developed. These meetings provide an opportunity to present one or more options to an individual, team or organization.

These meetings highlight a challenge or gap, and then offer an identified answer with a rationale around why this will address the unique need. This provides a valuable opportunity for an organization to demonstrate what they can offer a potential new client to gain new business. Solution-based meetings also demonstrate to leadership how a new project, product or service could benefit the organization.

Promoting and selling

Working

A working meeting brings participants together *to actively work through specific tasks and activities*. This type of meeting is focused on *creating, developing, reviewing or finalizing* something, including:

• Presentations
• Reports
• Processes and workflows
• Detailed workplans
• Sketches and models
• Spreadsheets
• Databases
• Other documents

These tend to be operational meetings where a tangible outcome is expected.

Working meetings are valuable as they bring the right expertise to the table *to work through a task or plan*. It allows participants to collaborate and co-create something together that the team or organization requires and considers important.

Can meetings have multiple purposes?

In many cases, meetings can *incorporate two or more* of the above reasons. By knowing these in advance, this allows you to plan the details of the meeting appropriately. This directly impacts your ability to:

• Set the right objectives and expected outcomes
• Select the right people to have at the table
• Allocate enough time for the meeting discussions
• Develop your agenda to accommodate the multiple purposes

You may find you have a unique meeting purpose that is not listed in the categories above. The information here is *meant as a starting point to help you define your unique meeting purpose*. Make sure you can answer the essential question upfront around why you need a meeting. Once your purpose is clear, move on to the next phase of planning in **Step 1: Before the Meeting**. This *foundational step* will set you on the right path for an effective and productive meeting.

Step 1	Step 2	Step 3
Before	*During*	*After*

Determine Your Meeting Objectives and Expected Outcomes

While the purpose answers *why* you are pulling a meeting together, your objectives and expected outcomes determine *what you want to achieve.*

Your meeting objectives and expected outcomes allow you to:

- Set appropriate meeting goals
- Define what success looks like
- Measure to see if you reach what you plan to achieve

Identifying these in advance provides you with a good foundation for the planning activities of your meeting. This chapter aims to define meeting objectives and expected outcomes, guide you on how to set these for your meeting, and describe the importance of having them.

What is an objective?

An objective is *a specific target or goal you plan to achieve.* Identifying objectives provides you with valuable information to begin planning and organizing your meeting. Depending on what you want to accomplish, you can use this to determine your agenda, who should participate, what meeting format makes sense, the room layout, etc.

Objectives can be *quantitative or qualitative* in nature, and allow you to measure if they are accomplished. When identifying objectives for your meeting, select statements that are *specific, tangible and achievable*. They should clearly define what you are trying to accomplish by holding the meeting.

Once you have considered your objectives, use these as a guide to develop your list of expected outcomes.

What is an outcome?

An outcome is *an end result, product or service*. While an objective describes *what you want to accomplish,* an outcome describes *what you did accomplish.* Without any outcomes, a meeting is ineffective and unproductive.

Expected outcomes provide you with a baseline to measure your success. Use your expected outcomes to plan the details of your meeting. Then, after the meeting is complete, compare your actual results against this vision of success.

Your expected outcomes allow you to set expectations early on with your participants. Before the meeting even takes place, use these to state what results you are expecting from your time together.

How do I define the objectives and expected outcomes for a meeting?

Ask several questions to begin identifying what objectives and expected outcomes should be set for your meeting. One important thing to note is that *objectives and outcomes are linked together.* Your expected outcomes should be directly tied to your objectives.

When defining your *objectives*, ask the following questions:

• What is the purpose of this meeting?
• What do I want this meeting to achieve?
• What are the meeting goals?
• What do I hope to get out of the meeting?

Develop one or more *specific and measurable statements* that outline your objectives. Start your statement with an action verb that describes what you want to do. Here are a few examples to choose from:

Assess	Establish
Build	Identify
Create	Improve
Compare	Increase
Decrease	Plan
Define	Prepare
Design	Reduce
Determine	Select

When defining your *expected outcomes*, ask the following questions:

• If the meeting goals are realized, what would that look like?
• What tangible results do I want to see?
• If this meeting was successful, how would I know?
• Do the expected results link directly to the meeting objectives?

Your expected outcomes will allow you to *measure the success and effectiveness of your meeting*. Sometimes there are valid reasons for not achieving all identified expected outcomes during a meeting. However, you should do your best to set realistic, attainable goals upfront and then plan the meeting to set yourself up for success.

Following your meeting, plan to circle back and evaluate if you achieved what you initially set out to accomplish. See if your *expected* outcomes become your *actual* outcomes.

To help illustrate this important activity, here are several meeting examples with the objectives and expected outcomes identified:

Meeting #1: You have identified the need to hold an **education** meeting.

---

*Scenario: You know you want to bring all the staff together to complete a **mandatory, one-hour health and safety training session**. This education will be provided by your organization's Occupational Health and Safety Department. Based on the size of your staff, you may need to break it up into several sessions. You still need to determine who should be at each session, where and when it will be held, etc.*

You identify the following objectives:

• Increase the awareness and understanding of the health and safety policies and procedures.
• Achieve a passing grade on the five-question quiz at the end of the session by all staff.
• Confirm that 100% of staff attend and complete this mandatory training by the end of the quarter.

Based on the objectives above, your expected outcomes include:

• All the staff understands the health and safety policies and procedures.
• All the staff passes the quiz.
• All the staff completes the mandatory training.

Meeting #2: You have identified the need to hold an **information-sharing** meeting.

> *Scenario: You have a **new initiative about to kick off**. You know you want to bring everyone who will be directly or indirectly impacted together to hear about this work. There is some information already available that will be valuable to share. You still need to determine who should be there, where and when it will be held, etc.*

You identify the following objectives:

• Achieve a shared understanding of the new initiative including the current challenges, goals, scope, target timeline, and baseline data.
• Determine who should participate on the project team to support the initiative.

Based on the objectives above, your expected outcomes include:

• Everyone impacted is aware of the new initiative and has the same understanding of what it's about and why it's moving forward.
• A list of names is generated with the participants for the project team.

Meeting #3: You have identified the need to hold a **needs assessment** meeting.

> *Scenario: A **new, potential customer** has reached out to you to gain the services of your company. You have some basic information from a brief, initial discussion. You both agree that a meeting is the next logical step to explore this relationship further. You still need to determine who should be there, where and when it will be held, etc.*

You identify the following objectives:

• Gain an understanding of the existing gaps or challenges this customer is experiencing.
• Define the customer's specific requirements to support the development of an appropriate solution.
• Clarify expectations around working together for the duration of the relationship including how frequently to meet, how to best contact each other, etc.

Based on the objectives above, your expected outcomes include:

• A list of existing gaps and challenges.
• A list of requirements to develop an appropriate solution.
• A shared understanding of how to best work together going forward.

Define a set of objectives and expected outcomes for every meeting you organize. This provides *valuable information* to plan the details of your meeting, and to *measure your success* after the meeting ends.

| Step 1 *Before* | Step 2 *During* | Step 3 *After* |

Identify the Right People to Invite

Have you ever participated in a meeting that *failed miserably because the right people weren't at the table*? The truth is, this frequently happens due to the following reasons:

• People are missed on the invite list (intentionally or not)
• A list of "must-have" participants is never identified
• The meeting time conflicts with other schedules
• The meeting is delegated inappropriately
• A key perspective isn't considered

This often leads to additional meetings to make up for the missing perspectives.

Identifying and inviting the right participants is essential to the success of your meeting. There are *several factors* that drive who should be included in the discussion.

This chapter will help you assess who to invite, how to determine your list of "must-haves," and how to manage your meeting if you can't get everyone there.

How do you determine who should be invited?

Selecting and inviting the appropriate participants is a *key success factor when planning your meeting*. Here are a few questions to consider when defining your meeting invite list:

• Who are the people or groups that are the **most knowledgeable** about your meeting topic?
• Who might **benefit from hearing the discussion** or any meeting presentations?
• Who has **direct responsibility or authority** for any decisions that need to be made?
• Who has **been involved in any discussions** around the meeting topic in the past?
• Who has **not been involved in any discussions** around the meeting topic in the past, but **should have been**?
• Who might be **influential** in the discussion and provide **experience and expertise** to support and guide the meeting?

When *determining who to invite*, consider the following additional factors:

• The meeting purpose
• The impact from the expected outcomes
• The level of involvement and support required

The meeting purpose

Your reason for holding the meeting provides great insight into who to include on your invite list. Use this as a starting point to define your participants.

- **Brainstorming** – Consider including *anyone who has a unique perspective* on the expected meeting topic. This is an opportunity to bring in others from different departments or services since this is typically a *one-time only* meeting.

  The more diverse the participants, the richer the discussion. You will benefit because the result will be a greater pool of knowledge about your meeting topic. Different perspectives are valuable for idea generation as they lead to *more robust results*.

- **Decision-making** – Think about *who has the authority* to make the decision. It might fall on one individual or it could be a collaborative approach requiring various perspectives. Identify who has *expertise that can understand and present the options* available to inform the discussion and the decision-making process.

- **Educating** – Determine if the education required is for *initial training, maintaining or upgrading skills, professional development, etc.* If the education needed is mandatory or out of interest, this should help you define your meeting invite list.

  For example, if you have several new hires in the past month and you need to offer initial training to new staff, use this information to define your invite list. Education meetings can include *specific individuals, entire teams or everyone* in your organization, depending on the need.

- **Gaining buy-in** – Depending on whether the change requires buy-in from the front line, operational teams or at the corporate leadership level, use this as a guide to determine who to invite. *Assess who needs to support the change* and the level of endorsement required, and then select the appropriate participants.

- **Identifying and assessing needs** – Depending on what issues, challenges, gaps or requirements you are trying to assess, the participants should include those who are experiencing these gaps. Your invite list might include:

• Your own team or staff
• Your customers or clients
• The project sponsor or champion
• Any potential end users
• Your direct leader or manager
• The executive leadership team

Select the participants who have the *greatest understanding* of the gaps or needs you are trying to address.

- **Information-sharing** – Since this type of meeting offers an opportunity to inform participants of updates and changes, consider *who will benefit from hearing the information* you plan to share. If there is any likelihood that an individual will be impacted and might react emotionally to the information, make sure you add them to your invite list.

- **Planning** – Meetings that have a focus on planning are intended to plan the logistics or details of a project, workplan, program, etc. Select individuals who offer *specific content expertise and knowledge related to the meeting topic*. Consider including various perspectives that will add value to the planning discussion.

- **Prioritizing** – Depending on whether the prioritization needed is at the *operational level or corporate, strategic level*, this will impact who you should include. Operational prioritization requires frontline management and staff, while strategic prioritization needs executive leadership attendance.

  Make sure you include individuals who offer an *understanding of the items being prioritized, what resources will be required and what level of effort is needed*. Include anyone who has decision-making authority and influence over the decision.

- **Promoting, selling and offering a new solution** – This meeting intends to offer a new idea, product or service in response to an identified need or gap. This will need to be presented to the *individuals who are experiencing the existing gaps and challenges*. Make sure the people you include have *decision-making authority* to accept the new solution.

  Include participants who can *promote and describe the new solution*, along with a rationale on why it's the best option. Have the right people with expertise included to answer questions as they arise.

- **Working** – Since this meeting focuses on working through a specific task or activity, consider who *offers content expertise* to support the discussion and the specific deliverable. These meetings typically consist of a small group who co-create and develop a tangible outcome.

The impact from the expected outcomes

Your expected outcomes will have an impact on individuals, teams, departments, organizations or potentially broader. The *level of impact could be measured* from low to high, and from direct to indirect. Use this as a guide to assess who to include on your invite list.

Low levels of impact include small, operational changes that have a minimal effect on staff and their daily activities. *High levels of impact* include broader, organization-wide changes that will be felt by many. The greater the impact of the expected outcomes, the more perspectives to consider including.

Individuals who are *directly impacted* by the expected outcomes will see a *measurable change* in either their environment, daily activities, workflows, etc. Select the appropriate people to include from this group. Others will be *indirectly impacted* and only require an awareness of the outcomes. This means the results will not tangibly affect them. Consider keeping this group informed through other means, such as email, internal websites, social media, etc.

Figure 5.1: Using impact to determine invite list

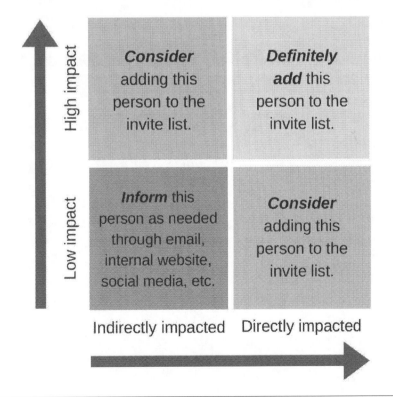

When identifying your invite list, consider the level of impact your expected outcomes will have on the various people within your organization, and potentially beyond.

The level of involvement and support required
Determine the involvement and support needed in your meeting. Participants could be there in a variety of different roles, such as:

• Decision-makers
• Content experts
• Champions or sponsors
• Workers or "doers"
• Influencers
• Learners
• Facilitators
• Reviewers
• Note-takers or scribes

Your meeting may need direct involvement of several of these supporting roles. Use this list to determine *who* to invite.

Why should you identify a list of "must-haves" for the meeting?

When taking all the possible participants into consideration, your invite list *may have become lengthy*. This is positive though as it demonstrates you have *considered everyone who might be required* based on your meeting purpose, impact, and required involvement.

Depending on the timeframe, competing priorities and challenging schedules, bringing everyone together on your invite list is not always realistic. This is where it is helpful *to identify a shorter "must-haves" list* that includes the individuals or groups you absolutely require to achieve your expected outcomes. While it may be ideal to have everyone on your list in attendance, you might find only specific participants *must be present*. The remaining invite list can be included, but if they are unable to attend, this won't prevent the meeting from being successful.

Take a few minutes and think about *who on your list is a "must-have"* and plan the meeting to make sure their attendance is possible.

What else can be considered if everyone can't attend?

Having all your invited participants present is not always possible. This could be due to:

• Scheduling conflicts
• Short notice
• Vacation time
• Distance and travel challenges

When finalizing your invite list, consider allowing delegation, connecting personally with those who can't be present, and organizing the meeting around industry-specific or seasonal factors.

Allowing delegation to others
If an invited participant is not going to be available, determine if it makes sense for that individual to *send an appropriate delegate in their place.* Identify why you need their perspective. If it's for decision-making, then specifically request they delegate the meeting to someone who has decision-making authority to support the discussion. If it's for information purposes, ask for a delegate and set the expectation they report the information back to the original invitee.

Connecting personally with unavailable participants
If an invited participant is unable to attend, *connect directly with that individual prior to the meeting.* This could be through email, hallway conversation, a quick phone call, etc. to gain their input and feedback. You can ask if there is anything they want you to share at the meeting on their behalf. A follow-up after the meeting may be required depending on the role of that individual.

Consider industry-specific or seasonal factors
There may be other considerations that impact your invited participants' availability. These could include:

> - **Industry-specific factors** such as annual conferences, teaching requirements, budget season, and customer, client and patient-dedicated time
> - **Busier times of day** such as first thing on a Monday morning
> - **Certain times of year** including over the summer and holiday seasons
> - **Other factors** that could impact availability and attendance

You will likely find there are certain times that work best. Think about any barriers to attendance, and then *organize your meeting to maximize the availability of your invite list*.

What happens if the right people aren't at the table?

Many existing resources around meeting management strongly suggest that by limiting the number of people in a room, this will result in more effective meetings. There are times when this is true. However, what is *absent in this advice* is that this solely *depends on whether the meeting discussion has an impact beyond the smaller group*.

A key perspective missed could *directly impact the outcomes* of the meeting. If relevant information is not readily available to support decision-making, or if the right expertise is not at the table to provide input, this could result in *push back, lack of buy-in and rework* after the meeting.

Meetings commonly take place without the right people at the table. This is because key participants from other departments, units, groups, and organizations are not taken into consideration during this stage of meeting planning. Decisions made by one group can *have direct, ripple effects beyond their group* and have dramatic impacts on others without even realizing it. A siloed approach to who is invited can have unexpected, negative consequences.

To mitigate any challenges from not having the right people at the table, complete a *thoughtful analysis of who will add value to the discussion*. Once again, explore your meeting purpose, level of impact, and the required involvement and support to help guide you in developing a comprehensive meeting invite list.

Chapter 6

Step 1
Before

Step 2
During

Step 3
After

Determine the Meeting Format

Have you ever attended a meeting by phone but would have benefitted from being in the same room? Have you ever traveled for a meeting that could have been done virtually? Determining the right format can impact how effective your meeting will be. The format describes *how you bring your participants together*.

There are a *variety of format options available* to you. Each has a different set-up, technology requirement and engagement strategy. There are pros and cons to each of these.

The *most common formats* include in-person, teleconference, web-conference and video-conference. A hybrid of two or more formats is often selected based on the needs and situation of each meeting.

Consider the following when selecting the format that makes sense for your meeting:

• The purpose of the meeting
• The objectives and expected outcomes
• The participants you are inviting
• The location of your participants

In-person meeting

What is an in-person meeting?
An in-person meeting *brings all your participants together in one room*. This format will always be the most engaging way to interact with everyone.

What are the pros and cons of an in-person meeting?

There are significant benefits to meeting face-to-face with your participants. In-person is *optimal for communication* since the words spoken, tone and body language can all be factored in.

Another advantage is the in-person interaction allows for *greater relationship building* than any other format. When you can place a face to a name, it is far easier to build a rapport and sense of trust with each other.

Following along with presentations and documents is easy during an in-person meeting as you will always have a *visual cue* to turn a page or see a slide change on a screen or monitor.

This format provides you with the opportunity to continuously scan the room to:

• Monitor the level of engagement from each participant
• Determine the overall energy of the group
• Read the facial expressions and body language of those in the room

The challenge is when participants are *not geographically co-located,* and travel is not feasible, or difficult due to time-constraints. If you have ongoing meetings, try to hold at least the first meeting in-person, if possible, to allow for that initial, face-to-face interaction and then consider other formats going forward.

When should an in-person format be used?
Select this format when your participants are either *located in the same area* and can come together in one place, or *when travel plans can be coordinated*. Certain meeting types are best done in-person. When the purpose of the meeting includes brainstorming, gaining buy-in, assessing needs and requirements, planning and working together, try to have all participants come together in the same room.

Teleconference meeting

What is a teleconference meeting?
Bringing people together in one room is not always possible or necessary. A teleconference meeting is *when all participants join a meeting by phone.*

Meetings done through teleconference can be very effective. However, there are additional considerations related to this format. It takes *significantly more effort* on the part of the meeting lead to properly engage the participants, and maintain a high level of engagement. Since the participants are not visible, it becomes more challenging to see if they are listening, multi-tasking or focusing on other, non-meeting related activities.

What are the pros and cons of a teleconference meeting?

Participants *from anywhere can join a meeting* discussion using a simple telephone, and potentially a teleconference phone line. Meetings done by phone require you to be *completely reliant on technology* to bring your group together. If your meeting consists of only two people, one person can call the other at the defined time through a regular phone line.

As soon as you add more participants, the appropriate teleconferencing resources are required. This includes *a pre-planned teleconference line* that all participants can dial into at the beginning of the meeting.

Although this allows multiple people to join a conversation at once, some challenges can unexpectedly, although infrequently, occur. There are times when the *service experiences technical difficulties* and the teleconference line doesn't work. Or, there may be *unexpected restrictions on the number of participants* allowed on the teleconference line, preventing some callers from gaining access if you have a large group.

All visual cues that come with reading *facial expressions and body language are non-existent* with this format. Special attention is required to listen to the words spoken and the tone of voice. The meeting lead should regularly check in verbally with members of the group to engage them and to gain their input.

Visual cues are also missing when *changing pages or slides* and should be clearly communicated to those on the phone.

When should a teleconference format be used?

Use a teleconference to meet if your participants are spread out geographically or for meetings that are *expected to be short* in duration. Consider a teleconference meeting for small, operational decision-making, information-sharing, problem-solving, and planning.

Chapter 15: Lead the Meeting Discussion offers several strategies around leading effective teleconference meetings to keep your group successfully engaged.

Web-conferencing meeting

What is a web-conference meeting?

A web-conference is *a meeting held virtually through the internet where all the participants connect in remotely through their personal computers.* Web-conferencing can be done from anywhere and is more dynamic and interactive than the teleconference format option.

This format includes an audio component. Typically, a teleconference line or audio through the computer is needed. This allows participants to communicate with each other or listen in on a presentation.

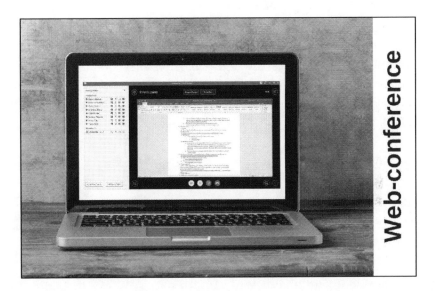

What are the pros and cons of a web-conference meeting?

Web-conferencing provides a *virtual environment* where meeting participants *can all view the same information* on their computer screens. This is shared by a presenter, often the meeting lead, where the presenter can be changed at any time.

This offers a *great, collaborative approach* as participants can provide input on documents presented on their screens. Any changes are visible in real-time.

Web-conferencing typically offers a *chat messaging* feature. This allows participants to communicate their questions or comments to the group and meeting lead during a presentation.

When should a web-conference format be used?

This format allows many people to *work collaboratively together* when there is distance between them. This can *reduce travel costs* significantly. Participants are able to join into a web-conference from anywhere in the world.

Web-conferencing provides an *ideal learning and training environment,* using webinars (web-based seminars). Consider this option for education meetings. This format also works well for information-sharing, planning and promoting new products, services, and solutions.

Video-conferencing meeting

What is a video-conference meeting?

A video-conference is *a meeting where participants are connected virtually through video and audio.* Video-conference meetings add an additional layer to the dynamic, virtual meeting environment. This format *adds a face-to-face component* to the communication.

This is typically through two-way video and audio connections, and between two or more locations.

What are the pros and cons of a video-conference meeting?

Video-conferences provide the *benefit of a visual connection* between participants. The *functionality of web-conferencing* is included where screen sharing is possible, allowing the presentation of information and team collaboration over distances.

With video-conferencing, there is the benefit of monitoring facial expressions and body language. However, there are limitations to this. You will *only see what is in view of the camera.*

A challenge with video-conferencing is there is a greater likelihood of technology glitches with this format. Depending on the setup, the internet connection, the room acoustics with microphones and speakers, etc., there is a greater risk of issues. If you are using this option, make sure you have someone technologically savvy to assist and to troubleshoot any unexpected challenges, should they arise.

When should a video-conference format be used?
This format has many practical applications in a variety of industries. Some examples include:

• **Telemedicine** - Physicians and other health care providers can provide consultation with their patients from different locations
• **Interviews** – Candidates can be interviewed over distances
• **Consultations** – Consultants can work with clients in service-based industries
• **Education** – Students can be taught through online classes

The possibilities are endless, and this meeting format can promote and drive innovation in many unique ways.

Hybrid Meetings

There are often times when meetings will incorporate two or more formats to accommodate the needs of all participants. For example, in-person meetings will often add a teleconference line allowing individuals to participate even if they are not physically able to attend. Another example is when two or more separate in-person meeting rooms, each with multiple participants in attendance, are connected visually through video-conferencing.

There are many creative ways to bring people together using a variety of the above formats. By identifying the needs of your meeting and the ability of everyone to attend, select from the options you have available to effectively engage the group and to achieve your expected outcomes.

Chapter 7

Step 1
Before

Step 2
During

Step 3
After

Identify the Meeting Logistics

One of the key activities when organizing a meeting is to identify the necessary logistics. The logistics define *when and where a meeting will take place*. This information needs to be well-organized before a meeting can be booked.

During this activity, you will plan a number of the meeting details. These include:

• The meeting **date**
• The meeting **time** and **duration**
• The meeting **location** and **room**
• The **teleconference, web-conference or video-conference** details
• The **food** and **drinks** (if needed)

Sorting out the *logistics is a prerequisite to booking a meeting*. This chapter will outline each of the necessary logistics and the important considerations of each.

The meeting date

The meeting date is the *calendar day identified to hold a meeting*. The date can be determined in two possible ways:

1. By planning the meeting around a **specific timeframe**
2. By planning the meeting around the **availability of your participants**

Planning around a specific timeframe

In many cases, a meeting date is *driven by specific business activities and timelines*. You may have a deadline to complete a task. The date you select should accommodate you with enough time to make the identified timeframe.

For example, if you know a new workflow process needs to go live by next Friday, then you need to book a training session before next Thursday, so everyone is prepared for the change. This provides you with a specific timeframe to select your meeting date from.

Planning around the availability of your participants

Another approach to consider is organizing your meeting around the *availability of your invite list*. The meeting date would be selected by investigating everyone's schedule and identifying a date that works best.

It's important to note that schedules won't always align perfectly. This is when you would *leverage your list of "must-have" participants* and look for a date that works specifically for this group. The meeting appointment would be circulated to everyone. However, you would be most concerned with the availability of your "must-haves."

The meeting time and duration

The meeting time and duration is *the time of day a meeting takes place and the length of time required to achieve the expected outcomes*. This takes into consideration:

• The best time of day
• The meeting start time
• The amount of time required
• The meeting end time

The best time of day
The time of day may be something to consider depending on your industry and the people you are inviting. Some professions and occupations have their busiest commitments first thing in the morning, while others are towards the end of the day. *Book your meeting around their availability* to provide them the best opportunity to attend.

For example, if you work in the health care industry and your invited participants consist of health care providers, including physicians, you don't want to interfere with time dedicated to patient care. If physicians are expected to attend, meetings should be organized around their availability. This is often very early in the morning or into the evening hours.

Consider the time of day if any of your participants require *travel time* to attend. Determine if they are coming from different locations and consider how to make it easier for them to attend. Sometimes selecting the beginning or end of day is easiest, especially if they have to be at their own work location on the same day.

The meeting start time
When defining your meeting logistics, determine what time you prefer to start the meeting. Select this time *based on the best time of day* to allow the greatest attendance from your invited participants.

The amount of time required
Although your detailed agenda is not yet prepared, you can still *estimate how much time you need* based on the meeting purpose, objectives and your expected outcomes.

Meetings can range from a few minutes to a full day, but typically fall somewhere in between. Estimate if you can accomplish your expected outcomes in 15 minutes, an hour or two, half a day or longer.

Consider the complexity of the discussion needed. For more detailed, complex discussions, allocate enough time for your participants to successfully contribute to the meeting.

The meeting end time

Once you define the best time of day, the meeting start time and the amount of time you need to achieve your expected outcomes, you can then *determine what your meeting end time should be.*

For example, if you know first thing in the morning this coming Friday will be the best time to bring everyone together, you then select 8:30 am to start the meeting. Based on your meeting purpose and objectives, you estimate it will take about an hour to achieve your expected outcomes. From this information, you determine your meeting end time should be 9:30 am.

The meeting location

The location is the *place where the meeting occurs* when holding an in-person meeting.

Selecting a meeting location

In some cases, the location selection is easy when all invited participants are *co-located in the same place*. However, when your participants are in different buildings, organizations, cities or even countries, the meeting location is often defined based on the following:

• Where the **majority** of the invited participants are **located**
• A **centrally located space** to make it manageable for everyone
• A **rotation of locations** (if multiple meetings are needed) to minimize the same people needing to travel every time
• The **need to use other meeting formats** such as teleconference, web-conference and video-conference

Holding off-site meetings

Another consideration is whether you want to *hold your meeting off-site instead of within the walls of your own organization*. Use this option when you don't have adequate meeting space available or if you want to provide a new, fresh environment for the discussion.

For example, if you are hosting a strategic planning session or a staff retreat, you might consider an external location. This helps the group think creatively and provides you with the space needed to fit your invite list.

Off-site meetings tend to have additional costs due to space rental, catering, audiovisual equipment rental, etc., so make sure you budget accordingly.

The meeting room

Meeting rooms come in a *variety of shapes and sizes* with nearly an *unlimited assortment of seating arrangements*. The purpose of your meeting can provide insight into the size of the room needed. Consider the number of people you expect to attend based on your invite list and book the appropriate room in advance.

The size of the meeting room
The room and space requirements will differ considerably when you have a meeting that has:

• Two participants (one-on-one meeting)
• A small group of 3-6 participants
• A medium group of 7 participants or more
• A large group of 20 participants or more
• A very large group of 50 participants or more

Determine if you will need enough space for your participants to *move around the room* or if you need space to *include any tools and resources* such as easels and flip charts, projectors, etc.

Think about what rooms you have access to in your organization. You will need a room that will hold the size of your group comfortably.

When considering your meeting room, determine if there are *any special accessibility needs* that should be accommodated based on your meeting invites.

Booking the meeting room

Once you identify what size of room you need, explore *what rooms are available on the selected date and time* for your meeting. Depending on your organization's internal room booking process, follow those steps to secure the room for your desired date and time.

If by chance you are booking an off-site meeting, contact the hosting site where the meeting will be held and place a hold for the desired room. If you are renting space, be prepared to pay at least a portion of the cost for holding the space.

The teleconference, web-conference or video-conference details

Depending on your selected meeting format, you may or may not need a physical meeting room. If your meeting format requires a technology component to bring your participants together, *book these resources at this time.* You can do this by first identifying what resources you have access to within your organization.

For example, you may have access to one teleconference line that is a *bookable resource*, or you may have *your own dedicated teleconference line* you can use at any time. For web or video-conferencing, take into consideration if your organization has purchased an *enterprise license* for any specific system for their employees to use for meeting management.

Once you identify what you have access to, book and secure these resources as needed. *Track the details* including phone numbers, passcodes, confirmation numbers or any other relevant information. Capture this information as this will be necessary to share when developing your meeting appointment.

The food and drinks (if needed)

While this is not always a requirement, there may be times when providing food and drinks (or coffee, tea, and water) for your participants makes sense. This is based on:

• The time of day
• The length of the meeting
• Your organization's business policies and budget

The time of day
If your meeting is planned for early in the morning, over the lunch hour, or into the evening, *consider if you will provide food and drinks* or if you will recommend that invited participants *bring their own*. If participants need to supply their own, make sure this is clearly communicated when you develop your meeting appointment.

The length of the meeting
Shorter meetings are less likely to include food and drinks. However, *longer meetings* that are scheduled half a day or longer may consider including drinks at the very least.

Your organization's business policies and budget
Some organizations intentionally include the availability of food and drinks for meetings. This might be *built within their policies,* and a budget could be set for this every year. However, this will look very different depending on whether you work for a *for-profit vs. non-profit organization, the size of your business, and the overall budget* you have to work from.

Providing food and drinks is often a tricky subject. Never assume that every meeting must offer these. This is *not a mandatory requirement* and requires careful consideration.

Before booking any food and drinks, check with your organization's leadership to determine the *appropriateness and the process* to include this in your upcoming meeting. You will also need to determine if you need to pick something up and bring it in on your own, if your organization has internal catering available or if they have a preferred caterer with an existing pricing arrangement.

When ordering food, don't forget to *consider any special dietary restrictions* such as allergies (ex. gluten free) and vegetarian options.

Step 1	Step 2	Step 3
Before	*During*	*After*

Develop and Circulate a Meeting Appointment

Before a meeting can take place, an appointment needs to be developed and circulated to your invite list. A meeting appointment is *an invitation that communicates to your invited participants that a meeting is being booked* and lets them know their attendance is requested and expected.

For a meeting to be secured in calendars, the logistics need to be prepared in advance. Once these are in place, the meeting can be booked. This is done by creating an appointment (or multiple appointments, if needed) and then circulating this out, usually through email. The appointment *places a hold in calendars* that informs your invited participants you are *requesting they prioritize your meeting over other activities* during that timeframe.

This chapter will outline what is needed to book an appointment, what information you should consider adding and who you should include.

What is needed to develop a meeting appointment?

To create a meeting appointment, you should have already identified the following:

1.	The meeting purpose, objectives, and expected outcomes
2.	The list of meeting invites including your "must-haves"
3.	The meeting format (in person, teleconference, etc.)
4.	The meeting date
5.	The meeting time and duration
6.	The meeting location and room
7.	The teleconference, web-conference or video-conference details

Once you identify the details above, you can create a meeting appointment. Develop a *clear subject line and any meeting content to place within the body of the appointment.* This information is essential to provide context-setting around the meeting purpose and to set expectations around attendance and participation.

Develop a clear subject line

The subject line of an appointment should *clearly describe what the meeting is about* using only a few, short words. The meeting purpose should be immediately apparent to your invited participants when the appointment shows up in their email and on their calendar.

Too often the subject line is *left generic.* This leaves everyone unclear of the importance of the meeting. For those who have their calendars filled with appointments, and in some cases are double or triple-booked, they will benefit from understanding the intent of your meeting at a quick glance.

Here are some examples of **unclear** appointment subject lines:

• Training Session
• Project Review Meeting
• Contract Review
• Budget Meeting
• Check-In Meeting
• Status Update Meeting

The examples above *only provide a glimpse* of what the meeting is about. The people you are inviting are involved in a variety of business activities and have many competing priorities. The *greater clarity* you can provide upfront will *increase the likelihood your invited participants will prioritize your meeting* over other activities during that time.

Here are some examples of **clear** appointment subject lines:

• New HR Recruitment Program Planning Session
• Monthly Sales Review Meeting
• Strategic Planning Kick-off Meeting

• Requirements Gathering Meeting for Financial Software
• Equipment Service Contract - RFP Planning Meeting
• Mandatory Health and Safety Training Session

The examples above use only a few additional words but immediately provide a greater sense of the meeting's intent.

Add content to the body of the appointment

Meeting appointments *should never be circulated without any information* in the body of the message. Provide enough information early on for your participants to be prepared.

Include enough content within the body of the appointment to identify:

• The purpose of the meeting
• The expectations around attendance
• The responsibilities of the participants

There should always be at least a few lines or bullet points of information included. *The consequences of an empty message* in the appointment may include *low attendance, blank stares* when the meeting starts, and *limited outcomes* from the meeting.

Figure 8.1: Empty Meeting Appointment

Subject: Status Update Meeting
Details:

If you received the empty appointment above, you might ask yourself the following three questions:

• What is this meeting about?
• Do I need to be there?
• Do I need to prepare anything in advance?

If you can't decipher the full context of the meeting above, then your invited participants would experience the same challenge.

Below are two examples of what could be included in the body of your meeting appointment.

Figure 8.2: New Meeting Appointment Example 1

Subject: RFP Scoring Tool Instruction Session
Details: This meeting is being placed in your calendar to bring all the Request for Proposal (RFP) evaluators together before we start to score the vendor submissions. During this time, we will be reviewing the RFP scoring tool, discussing expectations as an evaluator and answering any questions you have before the evaluation process begins. Please make every effort to attend this meeting. This will be done through web-conference. Click on the link below and dial into the audio call-in number to participate. A detailed agenda will be circulated before the meeting.

Figure 8.3: New Meeting Appointment Example 2

Subject: Call Center Dashboard Development Meeting
Details: In follow-up to a recent discussion around the need to develop metrics for the new call center, we are bringing this group back together to brainstorm the key metrics and indicators we will use to **develop the call center dashboard** for tracking our progress. We will use the boardroom, but have added a teleconference line in case anyone can't attend in person. Further information will be sent out shortly.

Can the meeting appointment be delegated to others?

Meeting delegation is *when an appointment is forwarded to include someone to extend the invitation or to replace attendance with another.* Occasionally, there are times when this is acceptable and should be encouraged. However, this is not always the case and should only be done when appropriate. These expectations can be placed within the details of the appointment.

Figure 8.4 New Meeting Appointment Inviting Delegation

Subject: Strategic Plan Announcement Meeting

Details:
We are pulling this large group together to announce our new strategic plan. This meeting includes leaders and staff from across the organization, and we encourage you to delegate this meeting to all members of your team.

Our new mission, vision, and values have been attached, and we will discuss our next steps and how everyone can participate going forward.

Another example is when a manager is unable to attend an information-sharing meeting and identifies a member of their team to participate in their place. This is with the expectation they report back on the discussion.

There are many meetings that *should not be delegated*. This includes discussions when *sensitive information* is discussed or when you need to *have the right decision-makers* at the table. If you want your invited participants to attend and not delegate the appointment to others, you may want to specify this clearly in the body of the message.

What if changes to the meeting appointment are needed?

A variety of situations could arise that result in the need to edit the details of a meeting appointment. This includes the need to change the scheduled day, time of the meeting, list of invited participants, location, etc. Periodically, circumstances may also require you to cancel a meeting appointment.

If you are resending an appointment, you can avoid confusion of sending multiple invites by editing the appointment subject line to reflect the changes you make. As an example, a change to the meeting room location can be revised from "Strategic Plan Announcement Meeting" to "NEW LOCATION: Strategic Plan Announcement Meeting."

Figure 8.5 Edited Meeting Appointment

Subject: NEW LOCATION: Strategic Planning Announcement Meeting
Details: *PLEASE NOTE: We have moved this meeting from the Boardroom to the Auditorium.*   ─────────────────────────   Hi everyone,   We are pulling this large group together to announce our new strategic plan. This meeting includes leaders and staff from across the organization and we encourage you to delegate this meeting to other members of your team.

If you need to cancel a meeting, you should do the following:

• Retract the appointment to pull the meeting from everyone's calendar
• Circulate a short email to let everyone know the meeting has been canceled along with any planned, next steps

If you are working with more than one organization, an email is essential as the meeting appointment may not be removed automatically from their calendars. This is especially true if the other organization is using a different email system. Here is an example.

Figure 8.6 Canceled Meeting Appointment Email

Subject: CANCELED: New HR Recruitment Program Planning Meeting
Details: Please note that the upcoming meeting to begin working through the planning for the new HR recruitment program has been canceled. Due to identified budget constraints, this will be put on hold until our next fiscal year. **Please make sure the meeting is removed from your calendar on October 15th from 8:00 to 10:00 am.** Thank you for your understanding, and we will re-engage you when we restart this work again.

Who should be included in the meeting appointment?

Meeting appointments should *include all the individuals, groups, and organizations you identified on your invite list.* If your participants have any executive or administrative assistants, include them on the appointment.

In many cases, you may find it is the administrative assistant who manages the calendar of an individual you wish to include in your meeting. They are often empowered to accept and decline appointments but can often work with you to rearrange schedules to accommodate your meeting time. Learning the names of these assistants and building a relationship with them is always wise, as they hold the key to gaining meeting access to many managers and leaders in your organization.

Chapter 9

Step 1	Step 2	Step 3
Before	*During*	*After*

Develop an Agenda for Your Meeting

Running a meeting without an agenda is equivalent to driving in a new country and expecting to show up at your intended destination without directions, a map, or GPS. *Agendas are your roadmap for a meeting.* Never underestimate the importance of having one.

This chapter will take you through:

- What is an agenda and why you should have one
- The key elements to include
- How to set the agenda
- How formal to make the agenda
- How to best present and format the agenda

What is a meeting agenda?

An agenda is a *sequenced list of discussion topics that are intended to guide a conversation between two or more people*. This list provides a path for the discussion to make sure you hit on the key topics and points within the duration of your meeting. An agenda *maximizes the use of everyone's time* and helps the discussion to arrive at the expected outcomes. Hence, your agenda is your figurative *"road map"* to guide you to your expected destination.

Agendas are fundamental to holding effective meetings. They lay out your expectations around the sequenced conversation and provide you with a valuable tool to move the meeting forward.

What are the key elements to include in an agenda?

The items included in an agenda will vary based on the meeting purpose and the required discussion topics. However, there are *several, standard sections* that should always be present when structuring a well-developed agenda. These include:

- **The meeting logistics:** The very top of your agenda is where the details of your meeting are summarized for quick reference and identification.

- **The opening**: The beginning of your agenda should always include a welcome and high-level overview. This section offers context setting on why the meeting is taking place, what you hope to accomplish and how you plan to achieve it.

- **The main discussion:** The middle of the agenda is where the main discussion and dialogue takes place based on the selected agenda items. This section is unique and specific to the needs of each meeting.

- **The closing:** The end of the agenda provides an opportunity to wrap up the meeting. This includes summarizing the key points and decisions, reviewing any required action items and determining next steps.

Let's delve a little deeper into each of the above sections.

The meeting logistics
Add the basic information about your meeting at the top of your agenda. This includes:

• The **name** of the meeting and/or committee name
• The **date, time and duration** of the meeting
• The room **location** (and address, if needed)
• The **expected attendees** (your invited participants)
• Any known **regrets** (those that notified they would not be attending)

- Any **expected guests** (this is relevant if the meeting is part of an ongoing team or committee)

Here is an example of what your meeting logistics would look like at the top of your agenda.

Figure 9.1 Meeting Agenda Logistics Example

Patient Medication Reconciliation Project Team
December 2, 2019
2:30 to 4:00 pm
North Tower Building, Conference Room 12-200

Expected Attendees:
Regrets:

AGENDA

The opening

How you open the meeting sets the tone for the rest of the time you and your participants spend together.

- **Welcome and introductions:** Start by welcoming everyone and thanking them for coming. Ask everyone in the room and those on the phone to complete a roundtable of introductions. This allows everyone to know who they are interacting with, and helps you to track attendance.

- **High-level overview and meeting purpose:** Take a few minutes to review the agenda with the group and provide a brief overview of why everyone is coming together. This level sets the discussion and makes sure the group has the same understanding of the meeting purpose.

- **Set meeting expectations:** Lay out your expectations at the beginning to set the right tone for the meeting. This is where you would provide any ground rules for the discussion.

The main discussion

The middle of the agenda will depend on the reason for holding your meeting and should include the discussion topics you need to cover. There are several things to consider for this section, including:

- **The number of agenda items:** A good rule to creating agendas is to *limit the number of agenda items* to only a few, key discussion topics. This allows the group to remain focused and more likely to achieve the expected outcomes. For one-hour meetings, try to limit your agenda to *no more than three main discussion topics*. This provides sufficient time for discussion, questions, and decision-making.

  Consider the *level of complexity* of the discussion to determine the appropriate number of agenda items to include. If you have a large number of main discussion topics to add, consider extending the length of your meeting or break them up into multiple meetings.

- **The sequencing of agenda items:** Consider the sequence of the main agenda items and *prioritize them* to make sure there is a *logical flow to the discussion*. You may want to consider placing the most important items earlier on the agenda to avoid running out of time. Think about prioritizing any discussion topics that require group decision-making ahead of any items meant for information purposes only.

- **Allocating times to each agenda item:** *Allocate a length of time* for each agenda item. Use this to keep the meeting on track. As the time reserved for each discussion topic comes to an end, encourage your participants to bring the conversation to a conclusion by asking for any decisions, action items, and any other required follow-up.

  If the situation should arise where it does not make sense to end a detailed discussion, you can ask the group to pause briefly and prioritize the remaining items to determine what will be discussed, pushed to another meeting or held off-line.

- **Incorporating breaks:** Depending on the length of your meeting, *consider adding breaks to maintain the productivity* of the group. Meetings that are slightly longer than two and a half hours can include a two to five minutes stretch break. However, if a meeting is scheduled for a full morning or afternoon, build in 15 minutes to break mid-way.

  Breaks provide your participants with the opportunity to use the restroom, get up and stretch, grab a drink, check email, make a phone call, etc. This also offers everyone a brief mental break and allows them to refocus their energy on the agenda and discussion.

  For full day meetings, add a break in the morning, a longer break for lunch and another break in the afternoon.

The closing

How you close the meeting is equally important as the rest of the agenda. Build in time to properly close out the meeting. This includes summarizing the meeting, reviewing action items and discussing next steps.

- **Summarizing the meeting:** Depending on the length and complexity of the discussion, leave enough time at the end of the meeting to *sum up the key discussion points, decisions, and risks or issues* that are raised during the meeting.

- **Reviewing action items:** Review of all identified action items before closing the meeting. This provides a great opportunity to *remind everyone of the tasks* they have been assigned and reinforces expectations for after the meeting.

- **Discussing next steps:** Discuss the required *next steps that should follow once the meeting is complete.* This might include several tasks and activities, communications, additional meetings, offline discussions, etc.

Here is a sample of what your meeting agenda might look like when you add the key elements of the logistics, opening, main discussion and closing.

Figure 9.2: Meeting Agenda Example

Orange Star Monthly Staff Meeting
Tuesday, December 4, 2017
8:00 to 10:00 am
Boardroom, Rm C3-104

Expected Attendees: The Orange Star Team
Regrets: Oliver, Mohammad
Guests: Katie Joseph from the Communications Dept.

AGENDA

1. Welcome and Overview

2. Upcoming Holiday Vacation Schedule

3. New Online Social Media Policy Review

4. Presentation from Communications on Intranet Website Changes

5. Roundtable of Program Updates

6. Review and Next Steps

How are agenda items set for a meeting?

There are a few ways to set an agenda. This will depend on the needs of your meeting. Here are several questions to consider:

1.	What is the **purpose** of the meeting (planning, information sharing, education, decision-making, etc.)?
2.	What do you **want to accomplish** in that time frame?
3.	What **decisions** do you need to make?
4.	What **risks or issues** exist that you need to discuss?
5.	Do you require a **one-time only** meeting or is it a **standing, ongoing** team or committee meeting?
6.	Will you be the one to **drive the agenda topics**?
7.	Will you need to put a **call out for agenda items** from invited participants?

One-time only vs. ongoing meeting agendas

Whether you are holding a one-time only meeting or a meeting from an ongoing team or committee, this could influence some of the items added to your agenda. This may also impact who drives the topics added to the agenda.

- **One-time only meeting agendas:** Often the individual, group or organization setting up the meeting drives the topics listed on the agenda. These meetings *arise for a specific purpose*. When setting the agenda, make sure the main agenda items cover the topics that require group discussion and input.

- **Ongoing meeting agendas:** There are many reasons for groups to meet with a *pre-determined frequency* (weekly, monthly, quarterly, etc.) for a *defined length of time* or ongoing indefinitely. Committees are an example of this, and the agendas will often reflect this ongoing nature.

  These agendas are set in a variety of ways. If the group has a workplan already developed, the agenda items will relate to the current phase or stage of their plan. Other groups may put out a "call for agenda items" where a request is sent to the participants inviting them to identify what they want to bring forward. This callout is done far enough in advance with a deadline. This is to allow enough time to develop and circulate the agenda before the meeting.

  With ongoing meetings, agenda items are often a *continuation of previous meeting discussion topics*. Project teams are great examples of this. A group reconvenes regularly to continue the discussion about the planning and implementation of a defined project.

  For ongoing meetings, you may want to organize your agenda to place new agenda items separately from standing agenda items.

New vs. standing agenda items for ongoing meetings
Ongoing meetings have an additional element to consider when setting your agenda. As identified above, there are often agenda items that are carried over as a continuation of a previous discussion. These are called *standing* agenda items, and they differ from new items that are added for the first time.

- **Standing agenda items:** Standing agenda items *remain on every agenda*. They require some level of discussion at every meeting. This may be on an ongoing basis or for a defined period. Keep these agenda items listed every time you develop the agenda and sequence them appropriately with your other discussion topics. A review and approval of previous meeting minutes is an example of a standing agenda item.

- **New agenda items:** You will likely have agenda items that arise based on the time of year, the activities underway, an identified risk or challenge, or anything else that requires focused attention. These new items are *sometimes more time-sensitive*.

How should an agenda be formatted?

Based on the needs of your meeting and how formal you expect the discussion to be, there are a variety of ways to format and present your agenda.

You can decide if it makes sense to send it out as:

- **A paper-based or electronic handout:** A handout is the most commonly used format for an agenda and is ideal for any meeting, regardless of its size or formality.

- **An agenda presentation slide:** If you are using a presentation to guide the meeting, having the agenda embedded as a slide at the beginning of the presentation is an acceptable format.

- **An email with the agenda outlined in the message**: For small, informal groups, listing the agenda within the body of your email is sufficient, as your meeting participants can print off the email to follow along with.

Here are some examples of different agenda formats:

Figure 9.3 Agenda as a Paper-Based Handout

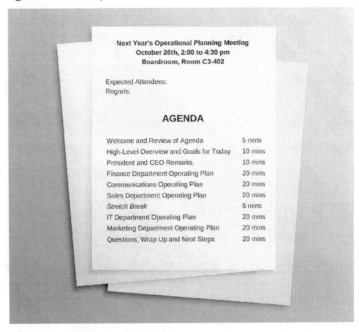

Figure 9.4 Agenda as a Presentation Slide

Figure: 9.5 Agenda Embedded in an Email

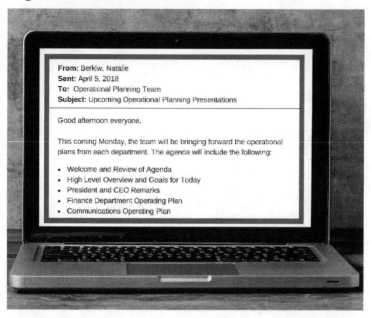

From: Berklw, Natalie
Sent: April 5, 2018
To: Operational Planning Team
Subject: Upcoming Operational Planning Presentations

Good afternoon everyone,

This coming Monday, the team will be bringing forward the operational plans from each department. The agenda will include the following:

- Welcome and Review of Agenda
- High Level Overview and Goals for Today
- President and CEO Remarks
- Finance Department Operating Plan
- Communications Operating Plan

How formal should an agenda be?

Meetings can range from *formal, structured discussions to informal conversations.* The formality of your meeting can impact how you choose to format your agenda and the level of detail to add.

Formal meetings typically have *more detailed agendas.* These include:

• The **discussion topics**
• A list of **sub-topics** (if applicable)
• The **most responsible participant** responsible to speak to each agenda item
• The **time allocated** for each discussion topic

A formal agenda is often structured into a paper-based format and circulated at the meeting, in addition to being sent by email in advance.

Less formal meetings also include the discussion topics and often identify the participant, but may be less concerned about the time allocation since the discussion is more casual. An informal agenda is sometimes provided as a handout, but may be sent within a presentation slide, in the body of a pre-meeting email, or within the details of a meeting appointment.

There are a few, additional things to consider when identifying how formal you should structure your agenda. These include the following:

- **The culture of your organization:** All your past experiences in your organization should give you a *sense of how structured or flexible most interactions are during meetings*. The environment and the expectations around formality are different in every organization.

  Think about the *typical work attire* in your environment. If everyone is wearing suits with ties, there is a good chance it is a more formal environment. Compare this to a workplace where jeans and casual clothes are the norms.

- **The number of participants:** The *number of participants* can drive how formal a meeting will be. Meetings with larger numbers of participants tend to *require greater structure* to keep the group on track. As the meeting invite list grows, you will benefit from a more formalized agenda. However, smaller groups (2-6 people) are more *conversational* and can often manage with a more informal agenda.

- **Who will be attending:** Consider *who you are inviting* to participate to determine how formal your agenda should be. Meetings that include members of your senior leadership team are more formal than meetings containing all front-line staff. If you expect participants from other groups or organizations, plan for a more formal agenda. Look at your invite list and identify what levels within your organization are attending to provide insight into how formal your meeting should be.

- **The meeting purpose:** The *reason* for your meeting can also influence how formal you should make your agenda. Information and working meetings are examples where less formal agendas tend to work well. On the other hand, meetings to promote a new product or service, or for decision-making are more formal in nature. Committee meetings also tend to be more formal in comparison to staff or team meetings.

Chapter 10

Step 1
Before

Step 2
During

Step 3
After

Determine the Room Layout

Meetings are all about *interaction and dialogue*. Setting up the room to provide the ideal conditions can dramatically *improve participation and engagement*. However, the needs of each meeting are unique and based on your meeting purpose, objectives and expected outcomes. If you are holding an in-person meeting, select a room layout that will set the stage for a successful meeting.

There are many creative ways to use the space to meet the needs of your meeting. This will depend on:

• The amount of space available
• The shape and dimensions of the room
• The number of participants
• The number, size, and shape of the tables available

While there are *unlimited ways to lay out a meeting room*, the most common room layouts include the following:

• Theatre or classroom style
• Boardroom style
• U or horseshoe style
• Group breakout style
• Face-to-face style

This chapter will review the different styles, and help you consider which layout to select.

Theatre or classroom style

This layout has everyone *facing in one direction towards the front* of the room. Tables may or may not be present depending on the purpose of the meeting. Generally, information is presented at the front. There may be whiteboards, flip charts, projector screens or other audiovisual equipment set up to support the content.

This style is *ideal for information sharing* when the information is *unidirectional*. Education meetings are also well-suited for this style. However, tables are a must for education purposes to allow participants to actively engage in the information. This is typically done through reference materials, handouts and note-taking.

This room layout is ideal for *large-sized groups* of participants. It's important to note there will be minimal collaboration and interaction with this style. Engaging in dialogue becomes difficult when everyone in the room is facing one direction.

Figure 10.1: Classroom style room layout

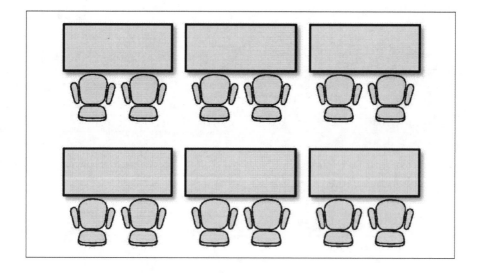

Boardroom style (Round, oval, square or rectangle)

This is a standard meeting room layout most people are used to. With this style, *everyone sits around a single table*. Participants can easily see each other around the room. This style is ideal for dialogue, interaction, and collaboration.

Meetings that would benefit from this layout include:

- **Working meetings** – Groups can come together to work through reports, presentations, plans, etc.

- **Planning meetings** – This could include project and planning teams developing a workplan, schedule, budget, risk management plan, etc.

- **Decision-making meetings** – Teams can come together to support a required decision.

- **Needs assessment meetings** - Questions can be asked to gain clarity and to understand gaps or challenges.

- **Information-sharing meetings** – This is ideal for information sharing that is *bidirectional* and when feedback is expected.

Consider this room layout for meetings with *small to medium-sized groups* to maximize the engagement of your participants.

Figure 10.2: Boardroom style room layout

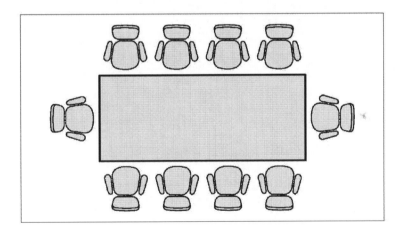

U or horseshoe style

A "U" or horseshoe shape layout is best to allow everyone to see each other, engage in active dialogue, and still face the front of a room. This style is *ideal for collaboration*. Someone is located at the front to capture the conversation or to present information that will be openly discussed. This combines the benefits of both classroom and boardroom styles.

This room layout is *a must for brainstorming meetings* where the group is facilitated. It allows everyone to *share information and bounce ideas off each other*. These ideas are captured at the front of the room using flip charts, sticky notes, whiteboards, etc.

Priority-setting meetings can also take advantage of this layout as options can be placed at the front. This allows the group to discuss how to best *prioritize activities, options, initiatives, and strategies.* In some cases, this is also ideal for education meetings. This is when there is an expectation the group will *openly discuss what they learn* throughout the session.

Medium-sized groups work well with this style as everyone will be able to see each other. To accommodate your participants, make sure the size of the room allows for the tables to be organized to seat everyone. The "U" shaped table should be expanded to fit all the participants comfortably.

Figure 10.3: U or horseshoe style room layout

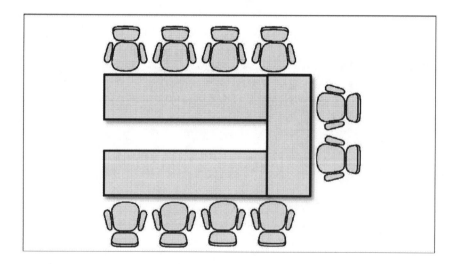

Group breakout style
This layout can look different based on the needs of your meeting. Multiple tables are *located around the room* to allow your participants to "*breakout*" into smaller groups for individual conversations. There may also be an element of table presentations and broader group discussion.

Many meeting retreats are organized using this room layout. The tables could be square, rectangular, or circular, and each will hold anywhere from 4-10 people.

This style is *ideal for large groups* where it makes sense to break up and work through detailed planning and structured exercises. Each group may need to present their table conversation to the larger room. This layout works well when trying to *develop large work plans* because the tables could be working on a different problem, task or idea, in unison, with various perspectives supporting the discussion.

Figure 10.4: Group breakout style room layout

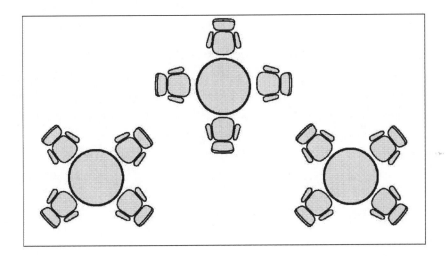

Face-to-face (across the table) style

Some meetings are small and will not require one of the above room layouts. Meetings between only two or three people have far more flexibility. They only need to find a space where they can face and engage each other effectively in discussion. A meeting room, coffee shop, sitting area or any other small area may be ideal.

This meeting style is ideal for *small groups* focused on gaining buy-in, assessing needs, information-sharing, planning and problem-solving.

Figure 10.5: Face-to-face style room layout

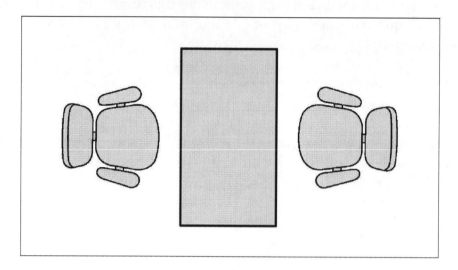

When selecting your room layout, take into consideration the purpose, objectives and expected outcomes, the number of participants, the room selected, and the table and chair options available. This simple consideration has a significant impact on the engagement of the group, and how effective the meeting discussion will be.

Step 1	Step 2	Step 3
Before	*During*	*After*

Determine the Resources and Tools You Need

There are *several, great meeting resources and tools available.* These can *enhance the discussion* and enable you to *capture, display and share essential information* during the meeting. Consider your meeting purpose, objectives, format and room layout, along with what you have available in your organization to select the most appropriate resources and tools.

The most *common resources and tools* used during meetings include:

• Audiovisual (AV) equipment
• Flip chart paper
• Handouts
• Laptops
• Markers
• Name cards, tents or badges
• Parking lot
• Presentations
• Sticky dots
• Sticky notes
• Whiteboards

This chapter will explore these resources and tools including what they are used for and any important considerations. Use this guide to explore what you have available to choose from, and what you may want to request to have on hand within your stock of supplies at the office.

What resources and tools are used in meetings?

There are a *variety of resources and tools* listed below to consider. Select what you need based on the unique needs of each meeting.

Audiovisual (AV) Equipment
There are a variety of resources that fall under the category of audiovisual equipment, often referred to as AV. Many meeting rooms *are already well-equipped* with these resources, and some workplaces offer these as *bookable resources* you can bring with you. The resources your organization might make available to you include:

• Cables for connection
• In-room computers
• Microphones and speakers
• Presentation clicker remotes
• Projectors and projector screens
• Teleconferencing phone systems
• Television monitors
• Video cameras

Here are a few questions to help you assess what AV equipment is needed:

• Will you be **projecting** slides or other information onto a **screen or television monitor** in the room?
• Will participants be **joining remotely** through teleconferencing, web-conferencing or video-conferencing?
• Will you be in a **large room** where it might be challenging for those in the back to hear?

If you will be *projecting information up on a screen or monitor*, you will need a room that already one of these built in. Consider if you need a projector, television monitor, in-room computer or laptop, and any cables for connecting to the screen or monitor for viewing.

If you have *participants joining remotely*, check to see if the room has at least a phone in the room with a speaker, video camera, in-room computer or laptop.

If you *are holding a larger meeting* including a retreat or conference, these are typically *held in large conference rooms* where the sound quality may be poor without AV equipment. AV is needed to project sound throughout the room. Consider if you need a microphone and speakers to enhance the sound of any speakers and presentations.

Don't forget to take into consideration your *technical knowledge* to set up the AV equipment, and to troubleshoot any challenges if they arise. Engage others with this expertise when needed.

Flip Chart Paper

There are a variety of ways to *capture information visually in the room*. Flip chart paper is a great way to keep your participants engaged as this allows them *to see their ideas documented as they are generated*. Place flip chart paper at the front of the room to track the meeting discussion. Also, place these around the room if you are holding any breakout group discussions.

Consider using flip chart paper when capturing the following:

• Action items along with who is accountable
• Brainstormed ideas
• Decisions made during the meeting
• Group feedback and input
• Key discussion points
• Off-topic issues raised for further discussion
• Risks and issues identified and any mitigating strategies

Flip Chart Paper

Some meeting rooms have easels with flip chart paper already set up. Other locations may have a place for them to be wall-mounted. If these options are not available, you can either tape sheets of flip chart paper up in the room or invest in large flip chart paper with adhesive backing that allows you to place them on the wall like a sticky note.

This resource provides an *engaging way to interact with your participants*. You can *capture their ideas in real-time* and continue to build on them together. This demonstrates that their ideas have been heard and were considered valuable enough to be documented for all to see.

Flip charts also offer an avenue for your participants to take on the role as scribe and track information on behalf of their colleagues.

Handouts

Paper-based handouts are still a valuable tool for meetings despite the ongoing move towards a digital world. These provide your participants with the *just-in-time information they can reference, fill out, or follow along with* during the meeting.

You can determine what handouts are most appropriate depending on the meeting purpose and the content to be discussed. Some common meeting handouts include:

• Agendas
• Annual reports
• Attendance sign-in sheets
• Breakout group exercises and instructions
• Datasheets and dashboards
• Financial documents and reports
• Meeting minutes from previous meetings
• Printed presentation slides with space for note-taking
• Strategic plan documents

Paper Handouts

You may want to include these handouts electronically before the meeting when you circulate your meeting communication and package. However, there may be times when you feel it's best to provide these documents at the start of the meeting.

Laptop

A personal laptop is a valuable resource that supports a variety of meeting activities, including:

• Connecting to a projector or monitor
• Capturing and documenting detailed meeting notes
• Setting up web-conferencing and video-conferencing meeting formats
• Looking up information in real-time if needed during the discussion

Laptops are a valuable resource for working meetings. If the group is working on a report, presentation, project plan, process map, or another document, a laptop *allows you to edit this work while the discussion takes place.*

Education meetings may require participants to have access to personal laptops. For example, a team training session to learn a new software system would require the participants to have their own individual computer to follow along with the learning.

Some organizations offer a designated computer lab with various computer stations specifically for training. Check to see if this is available and if not, ask your invited participants to bring their laptops. Don't forget to remind them to bring their power cords.

Markers

Markers are a simple, yet valuable tool for allowing you to capture information during a meeting. Depending on whether you are documenting the information on flip charts, sticky notes, whiteboards, etc., you can *select from an assortment of permanent or dry erase markers.*

The most common colors used include blue, black and red. However, there are many other color options to select from if you want to add some creativity to the group discussion.

When selecting markers to use, don't forget to consider the *point width as they can vary from very fine to a very thick point.* If you are in a large room, fine point markers may not be visible to those sitting across the table or at the back of the room. On the other hand, a very thick point marker will prevent you from capturing enough detail on smaller surface areas including sticky notes.

Name Cards, Tents or Badges

Displaying your participants' names is not always necessary, but you may occasionally hold a meeting where this is valuable. Formal committees, board meetings or large conference events where participants are coming from across your organization, or perhaps multiple organizations, *may benefit from displaying the names of everyone* at the table.

If your participants will be *collaborating with others, moving around and networking*, then name badges are ideal. However, in meeting rooms where the layout allows everyone to face each other such as round, oval or U-shaped tables, large-print name cards or tents placed at each seat will be far more beneficial.

Parking Lot

A parking lot is a tool used during facilitated meetings that provides a place to document generated *ideas or suggestions that are off-topic from the agenda*. The value of a parking lot is that it takes these ideas and visually documents them as a *commitment for future follow up* and offline conversations. This can be a great tool to refocus the group back to the intended discussion.

You can use other resources listed in this chapter as a parking lot. Capture your parking lot items on a visual resource such as flip chart paper, sticky notes or whiteboard.

Presentations

Presentations are a great tool to *visually communicate information* to your participants. These can be done in a variety of formats including slide decks, large display boards, printed posters, etc. Presentations are an effective way to highlight important information and *communicate key messages* to your participants.

Slides are the most commonly used tool for presenting, and there are various resources available to create dynamic presentations. These include, but are not limited to, Microsoft PowerPoint, Google Slides, Keynote for Apple, and Prezi.

Sticky Dots

Sticky dots come in a *variety of sizes and colors*. These can be a handy resource to support prioritization, sequencing, and decision-making. Once ideas or activities are documented on flip charts or sticky notes, colored sticky dots can be used by the meeting lead or the participants to *identify priorities or vote on key decisions*.

For example, you may identify a number of possible vision statements during a strategic planning session. By handing out several sticky dots to the participants, they have the opportunity to vote on their preferred statement. Those with the greatest number of sticky dots are considered to move forward.

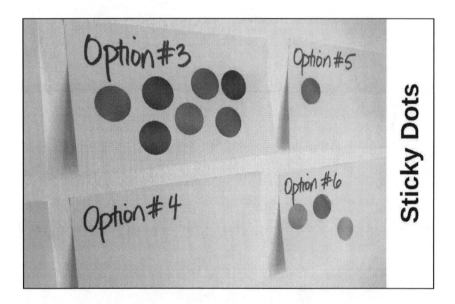

Sticky Notes

Sticky notes are a valuable resource that is often underutilized. Individual ideas and activities can be documented on each sticky note providing you with *incredible flexibility to shift and move the content* around as needed during the discussion.

If you are using sticky notes to capture ideas generated in a brainstorming session, then each sticky note would represent a different idea. These would be placed up at the front of the room. You have the flexibility to rearrange the placement of these sticky notes into different categories or along a timeline.

An important consideration when using sticky notes is the *wall surface* in the meeting room. Sticky notes require a flat surface and will not adhere to every wall. Even a slight texture may result in a random rainfall of sticky notes throughout your meeting. Whiteboards are smooth and provide a great location to place sticky notes. An alternative is to tape up several sheets of flip chart paper on the wall and use these to attach the sticky notes.

Whiteboards

Many meeting rooms have whiteboards installed on the walls. These provide you with an ideal location to:

• Write any key discussion points and ideas generated
• Place information captured on sticky notes
• Lay out your meeting expectations for the participants
• Provide instructions for group breakout discussions and exercises
• Capture off-topic ideas for further discussion in a parking lot
• Highlight housekeeping items such as WiFi passwords, restroom locations, contact information, etc.

There are a number of great resources and tools to assist you in leading an effective meeting. Find out what options your organization offers and select what makes sense for your specific meeting needs.

Step 1 *Before*	Step 2 *During*	Step 3 *After*

Develop and Circulate a Meeting Communication and Package

Participants often express frustration about *not feeling informed or prepared* when entering into a meeting and *unclear of what is expected of them* once they arrive. How often have you attended a meeting without any understanding of what would be discussed or how you needed to prepare in advance?

Some of the common challenges expressed include *not knowing*:

• Why the meeting is taking place
• Whether they really need to attend
• What the meeting is meant to accomplish
• What will be on the agenda for discussion
• What documents they should review in advance
• What else they need to do to prepare
• What will be expected from them at the meeting

After the planning is complete, you have the ideal opportunity to set the stage for a successful meeting by *actively communicating to the group*. This chapter will walk you through the importance of this activity, what to include, who to send this to, and when this should be completed by.

What is a meeting communication and package?

A meeting communication and package is *an important planning activity that communicates the important details about an upcoming meeting, and sets clear expectations with all individuals and groups invited.*

A meeting communication and package is typically *sent by email* and comes directly from, or on behalf of, the meeting lead.

This communication provides valuable information including:

• A high-level overview of the meeting purpose, objectives and expected outcomes
• The developed meeting agenda
• Any documents, presentations or other meeting materials that are attached
• Any expectations around how to prepare in advance
• Any expectations around what is required of them during the meeting
• Any other essential information (directions, if food is provided, etc.)

Creating a communication to your participants is the final step before the meeting takes place. More *detailed information is now available* to share compared to when you previously developed and circulated the meeting appointment.

Why is it important to send a meeting communication and package?

A meeting communication allows your participants to understand:

• Why the meeting is important
• What the meeting is about
• Why they need to attend
• What documents or presentations they should read in advance
• What documents they should develop or bring with them
• What pre-thinking they should do before the meeting

> - What role they need to play
> - What level of participation is required when they arrive

By circulating a meeting communication and package, you are *taking all reasonable steps* to actively communicate the meeting's intent, and to set clear expectations.

Don't worry if you already provided some of the same information in the meeting appointment. Take this opportunity to *reiterate what the meeting is about*, and expand on the details further. Your participants are involved in many different business activities and have a variety of competing priorities. It's always appreciated when additional effort is made to make sure they have all the information they need in advance.

What should be included in a meeting communication and package?

When developing your email, there are several key elements that should always be present. These include:

An introduction to the meeting
The first line of your email should identify what meeting you are referring to and reiterate the *meeting purpose*.

The objectives and expected outcomes
In one or two lines, state *what you hope to achieve* during your time together and what success will look like if the meeting goes well.

An overview of the agenda
Inform your participants *what you plan to discuss* during the meeting. Attach the agenda or include the agenda items within the body of the email.

A list of attached documents
Identify any *documents you are attaching* that will be discussed or referenced at the meeting. This includes any presentations, reports, spreadsheets, etc. If you have multiple items, it's best to list them out.

Set any expectations
Lay out your expectations around how your participants need to prepare and *what is expected of them* at the meeting.

The closing
Close out the communication by adding any final pleasantries and farewell greeting of your choice, your name, and contact information.

What expectations should be set in the meeting communication and package?

The expectations you set are unique to the needs of each meeting. Take this opportunity in your communication to state what you need from them. Select from any of the following or come up with your own based on your situation.

Before the meeting

• Read the attached materials in advance
• Bring the following items with you (documents, laptops, notebooks, etc.)
• Develop or create the following documents and bring them with you (status updates, presentations, reports, etc.)
• Complete some pre-thinking about an agenda topic before arriving
• Come with any questions about an agenda topic
• Delegate the meeting to others
• Don't delegate the meeting to others
• Fill out any needed information or templates before the meeting
• Provide any information or feedback in advance, if you can't attend
• Print out copies of the attached documents
• Printed copies will be made available at the meeting for you

During the meeting

• Arrive early, if possible
• Attend in person only
• Call into the meeting, if needed

• Drinks and/or food will be provided
• Bring your own drinks and/or food
• Be prepared to actively participate in the discussion
• Be prepared to actively listen (to any presentations, information-sharing, etc.)
• Come prepared to make any decisions
• Come with any questions
• Be prepared to provide an update on a previous action item
• Expect any guests at the meeting

What else should be considered when circulating a meeting communication?

Develop a clear subject line

When developing a communication to your invited participants, pay attention to the subject line of the email. This should *clearly describe what meeting the email refers to and what is included.* The subject line allows your participants to notice it when received, read it, and follow up on any expectations laid out for them.

Here are some examples of *clear subject lines* for the meeting communication and package:

• Agenda and Pre-Reading: Health & Safety Training Session
• Upcoming Scheduling Software RFP Meeting – Proposals Attached
• Monthly Staff Meeting: Agenda and Materials for Printing
• Draft Plan for Monday's Communication Plan Kick-Off
• AGENDA for Office Space Refresh Steering Committee Meeting

As you can see, there are a variety of ways to structure the subject line. Develop your subject line based on the unique needs of each meeting to clearly describe the purpose and provide a glimpse of what is included.

Add directions to the meeting (if needed)
If you are holding an in-person meeting, consider if any of your invited participants are coming from another location or organization. Unless they are all familiar with where the meeting will take place, add the directions to the meeting location and room.

Who should the meeting communication and package be sent to?

Make sure *everyone invited* to the meeting is on the list to receive the meeting communication and package. If additional participants are added to the invite after the meeting appointment is circulated, make sure they are included.

If your participants have executive or administrative assistants, include these individuals on the email *in the "cc" address line*. This is short for *carbon copy and means they receive a copy of the email,* even though it's not directly addressed to them. They often print documents and alert the participants of expected actions before the meeting takes place.

When should a meeting communication and package be sent out?

The earlier your participants have the information about the meeting, the better. While it's not always possible to send the meeting communication and package well in advance, *try to send it at least one day before* the meeting. This gives some time for your participants to read the email and review any materials in advance. If you send any documents right before the meeting, your participants will not have time to review them prior to attending.

However, if your participants are expected to come to the meeting having prepared any presentations, reports or other documents, *alert them as far in advance as possible.* The more time you can provide, the greater ability they have to build this activity into their busy schedules. Provide them with *adequate time to prepare.*

Depending on the *complexity* of any reports, presentations and other documents you need your participants to prepare for the meeting, determine if they need more than 24 hours' notice. Some documents and reports may actually require up to a week in certain situations to pull the right information and/or data together.

Figure 12.1: Meeting Communication and Package Example #1

Subject: Upcoming SUV Exterior Design Selection Meeting

Good afternoon everyone,

We need to begin the selection of the exterior SUV design for production. In advance of Thursday's meeting, here are some further details along with the agenda.

Our new Design Director will be attending to provide an overview of her expectations. During this time, we are going to review the designs and determine which ones will be most suitable for representing the brand. The leadership team will be voting on the submissions to be developed further.

The **agenda** will include the following:
- Welcome and Attendance
- Overview of Brand Expectations
- Presentation of Exterior Sketches
- Voting on Designs
- Finalizing a Singular Design Theme
- Next Steps

We will be meeting in the 2nd Floor Design Studio, Room 211B. The design sketches will be presented when you arrive. Come prepared to help us make a decision to allow us to meet our targeted timeframe.

Thanks, and see you Thursday.

Figure 12.2: Meeting Communication and Package Example #2

Subject: New Facility Opening Implementation Schedule Meeting

Good morning,

In advance of our upcoming implementation schedule planning meeting, I wanted to provide the group with some context-setting in advance.

The project team has reached a point where we need to sequence all the work we identified to open the new facility, and to start building the implementation schedule. We are pulling all of you together to assist us in brainstorming anything happening over the next few months that we need to take into consideration as we begin to assign dates to our project plan.

The **agenda** will include:
- An overview of what is within scope
- A review of the identified activities in the project plan
- A brainstorm on other projects and events that could impact our schedule
- Sequencing the activities and assigning dates
- Finalizing the implementation schedule

Please note that <u>lunch will be included</u>.

The **project plan is attached** for everyone to review prior to the meeting. Please come to the table having completed some pre-thinking around what other activities may have dependencies with this work or may impact the development of our schedule.

Thank you.

Step 2: *During* the Meeting

Chapter 13

Step 1	Step 2	Step 3
Before	*During*	*After*

Set Up Before the Meeting

As the meeting approaches, *make sure everything is in order* before it starts. There are several activities you should consider during the time leading up to the meeting. Provide yourself with *enough time to get everything prepared* and ready, and to *manage anything unexpected* that could arise.

These activities include the following:

• Print and photocopy any documents
• Add final touch-ups to presentations
• Gain early access to the meeting room, if in-person
• Organize the tables and chairs
• Consider the room temperature
• Adjust the lighting
• Prepare the required resources and tools
• Set up the audiovisual equipment
• Organize the drinks and food, if included

This chapter highlights the set-up activities outlined above, why they are important, and any contingency plans needed if something goes wrong.

What activities are needed to set up before a meeting?

Here is an overview of the various activities you should consider when setting up for the meeting and how to troubleshoot any challenges should they arise.

Print and photocopy any documents

Prior to the meeting, take some time to add any final touches to the documents that will be used or shared. If you are providing hard copies to your participants, take into consideration how many people you invited and create *enough copies for everyone*.

- **Contingency planning for printing and photocopying** - Once any handout materials are prepared and finalized, *print these well in advance* of the meeting, if possible. It's not uncommon for printers and photocopiers to *jam or run out of toner and ink*, only to bring your printing job to a halt. The last thing you want is to have an issue only moments before your meeting begins. By printing in advance, you mitigate this risk.

  As another contingency, identify if there is a *secondary printer or photocopier* close by you can redirect your printing to, if needed.

Add final touch-ups to presentations

If you plan to present slides at the meeting, *review them one last time*. Make any final edits and touch-ups as needed. Check to make sure the slides are:

• Not too text-heavy and maintain some white space in between
• Visually appealing with appropriate graphics, diagrams, fonts and bolding
• Sequenced appropriately to flow logically
• Clear on key messages, takeaways, and calls to action

- **Contingency planning for presentations** - Always *print out at least one copy* of the presentation slides before the meeting. If any issues arise with the audiovisual equipment, you can still follow along and talk to the slides to *minimize any interruption*.

Gain early access to the meeting room

If the meeting is in-person, check to see if you can access the meeting room in advance. Consider *adding an additional 15 minutes* to the room booking prior to the meeting, if the room is available. This gives you a little extra time to:

• Set up the room layout as needed
• Make sure the audiovisual equipment is up and running
• Organize your resources and tools in the room
• Set out any paper handouts

Organize the tables and chairs

Based on your selected room layout, consider if the meeting room is *already set up* as you need it or if you *need to rearrange the tables and chairs*. If rearrangement is required, gaining access to the room in advance as outlined above provides you with extra time to shift the tables around.

- **Contingency planning for organizing the tables and chairs** - There may be times when you enter a meeting room only to find that the previous group moved the tables and chairs around but failed to move them back where they belong. The extra time built in before the meeting will help mitigate this challenge should it arise.

  Always *find a second pair of hands* ready to help move any tables and chairs. This will minimize the risk of injuries from moving these heavy items yourself.

  Watch for the following *additional challenges* that could occur with the table and chairs. These include:

• Missing tables and chairs that were never returned
• Broken tables or chairs in the room
• Leftover handouts, food trays, trash, etc. from the previous meeting
• Requiring additional tables and chairs from what is already in the room

  Some rooms have tables that are unmovable, and this may eliminate some of the possible challenges. While some of the above issues are out of your control, leave enough time in advance to do what you can.

See if your organization allows you to *request any table and chair configurations* in advance when booking the meeting room. Also, order any additional tables needed before the meeting.

Be sure to report any missing or broken tables and chairs should these occur.

Consider the room temperature

While room temperature is often outside of your control, it's still something to take into consideration. The comfort of your meeting participants *can support or hinder their ability to remain focused* during the meeting.

The *time of year and any extreme temperature conditions outside* (hot or cold) can impact the temperature of a room. This is especially true for rooms with large windows and makes it more difficult to regulate the temperature. Also, larger groups of people can impact the temperature as *body heat will gradually warm the room*.

When setting up the room, check to see if there is an *adjustable thermostat* in the room, and open or close any windows, curtains, and blinds.

Consider checking in with your participants periodically during longer meetings to ask if the temperature is comfortable. Then consider adjusting as needed.

Adjust the lighting

The lighting is another important consideration when setting up the meeting room. The amount of light you need will vary depending on the needs of your meeting.

Presentation slides need a darker room environment. This allows everyone to see the projector screen or television monitor more clearly. However, you need to *balance this with some light*. A room that is too dark might result in your participants falling asleep.

Brighter rooms are ideal when you need the group to be actively engaged and creative. *Natural lighting is always best*, but not always possible. If there are windows, adjust the blinds or curtains appropriately. Consider *the time of day* since the sun may be low and blinding at the beginning or end of the day.

If there are multiple light switches in the room with fluorescent lighting, *try different combinations of the lights* to determine the ideal amount of light for your meeting.

Prepare the required resources and tools
Decide where in the room you need to place any resources and tools you plan to use. They should always be easily accessible. For example, flip chart paper and markers can be placed at the front or throughout the room.

- **Contingency planning for preparing the resources and tools** – Some of the unexpected issues that may arise include the following:

• The dry erase or flipchart markers in the room are dried out
• The wall surface is rough. Sticky notes won't adhere and begin raining down mid-meeting
• The flip chart easel only has one sheet of paper left, and you needed more
• Someone wrote on the whiteboard with permanent marker, and it won't erase

Prior to the meeting, check your flip chart paper and marker supplies. Always *keep an extra pad of flip chart paper, and extra permanent and dry erase markers.* Test out the markers periodically to see if they are drying out. Consider replacing them every few months if needed.

If using sticky notes to capture ideas, *test out the wall surfaces* in advance. Where there is any texture to the wall, your sticky notes will not adhere. Instead, use a whiteboard or flip chart paper as a more appropriate surface. Also, consider using *name brand sticky notes over generic* as they tend to have better adhesive qualities.

Any *damaged whiteboards should be immediately reported* for repair or replacement.

Set up the audiovisual equipment

Take the time needed when setting up to *make sure the audiovisual equipment is up and running*. This could include the teleconferencing, web conferencing and videoconferencing, projectors or television monitors, speakers and microphones, etc. This work often takes the longest to set up.

If you plan to present information upon a screen or monitor, set this up before the meeting starts. Load up any presentations or documents you want to present and make sure they are showing up clearly on the screen.

Call into the teleconference line *at least several minutes before the meeting*. This is to make sure the line is working before your participants begin logging into the call. If microphones need to be placed around the room for the teleconference, set these up as needed. If each seat is already outfitted with a microphone, make sure these are all turned on.

Web-conferencing and video-conferencing tend to require even more additional time for set up. Give yourself *plenty of extra time* prior to the meeting to set up the required equipment up in advance and test it out if possible.

- **Contingency planning for setting up the audiovisual equipment** - Audiovisual equipment can be challenging if it's not working properly and the right skill set to troubleshoot the challenges isn't present.

  Some *common teleconferencing problems* include:

• The teleconferencing system temporarily goes down
• The teleconference line details were sent out incorrectly
• The teleconference line has an unexpected maximum number of allowed participants
• The phone cord isn't long enough to bring the phone closer to the participants in the room
• The room unexpectedly has no phone at all

> • The unplugged speakerphone takes a considerable amount of time to re-set before you can begin using again

Some of these issues are outside of your control. Double-check the teleconference details previously circulated to make sure they are correct. Also, find out from your organization the maximum number of participants allowed on your teleconference line.

Consider checking to see what resources are available and their placement when you book the meeting room.

Some *common projecting and presenting problems* include:

• The laptop you are using is almost out of power
• The image on the screen is fuzzy or is unexpectedly turning blue, pink, green or another unexpected shade
• The room is missing a connection cord to plug your laptop into the projector or monitor
• The in-room computer needs a log-in name and password which are not clearly marked anywhere
• The presentation clicker to change slides is missing
• The remote to turn on the projector or monitor is missing or not working
• The file you saved to a memory stick is corrupted leaving you without a presentation

Always *carry a power cord* with you for your laptop. When setting up, make sure all *connection cords are tight and secure* to minimize the risk of issues when projecting. If you have an information technology (IT) team or someone in the office that is more technologically inclined, ask them for assistance when needed.

As discussed previously, always have at least one printed copy of your presentations on hand.

Report any significant issues for any necessary repairs or replacements.

Organize the drinks and food

While this is not always provided or necessary, there are some business environments or situations where drinks and food are included. This may include full-day meetings or those that fall over the breakfast, lunch or dinner hour.

Determine whether the drinks and food will be *placed inside or outside of the meeting room*. Place this where participants can help themselves while *minimizing disruptions* if someone gets up mid-meeting to refill their cup or plate.

- **Contingency planning for organizing the drinks and food** – Some challenges may arise when setting up any drinks and food for your meeting.

The *common drink and food problems* include:

• The caterer doesn't show up at all
• The food and drinks arrive late causing the meeting discussion to be disturbed
• The food is set up, but you quickly realize you are missing serving spoons, cups, plates, napkins or utensils
• There isn't an extra table set up anywhere to put the food and drinks on

If food and drinks will be catered in, *connect with the caterer within 24 hours* before the meeting to confirm delivery time. This makes sure they are prepared, and your order is in their queue. Also, keep a copy of the *caterer's phone number* with you in case you need to step outside and call.

When arranging the tables and chairs, organize these to make sure there is adequate space for laying out the drinks and food. *Order extra tables* if needed, or you may end up wandering the halls to find another table to pull in.

Provide sufficient time prior to the meeting to troubleshoot any unexpected issues that arise when setting up. Remember to *remain calm and breathe*. You are more likely to problem solve effectively if you remain cool and steady.

If the issue isn't resolved prior to your participants arriving, inform them calmly of any unexpected challenges. Explain how you will adjust the meeting to manage the issue. This demonstrates your flexibility and your participants will be impressed by your ability to keep calm under pressure.

Step 1	Step 2	Step 3
Before	*During*	*After*

Open the Meeting

A strong start to your meeting sets the *right tone upfront* and prepares your participants for an *engaging, effective discussion.* The first few minutes should include several, important opening activities. Too often these steps are accidentally missed or intentionally skipped over. Many meeting leads jump right into the agenda topics without taking the time to welcome the group and level set why the group has come together.

What steps are required to open a meeting?

Here are the activities you should follow to open the meeting:

• Welcome participants as they arrive
• Officially start the meeting
• Welcome everyone and thank them for coming
• Hold introductions and capture attendance
• Lay out the meeting purpose, objectives and expected outcomes
• Review the meeting agenda
• Set clear expectations for the meeting

These activities should *only take a few minutes* in total but are essential to opening the meeting effectively. You can find each of these steps outlined in further detail below.

Welcome participants as they arrive

Depending on the meeting format you selected, participants will begin joining you in the meeting room, on the phone, or virtually through web or video-conferencing. As they join, this is a *great time to welcome people*, introduce yourself and hold any casual conversations. Let the group know periodically that the meeting will start shortly.

If you are meeting in-person and have handouts, this is a great opportunity to begin handing them out or asking participants to pick them up on their way in.

Take this opportunity for *small conversation and building relationships* with your participants. Unstructured, friendly dialogue is welcoming and puts everyone at ease.

Officially start the meeting

Pay attention to the clock and start the meeting *as close to your scheduled start time as possible*. Some participants might be coming from other meetings or traveling, but don't let this stop you from getting the meeting going. You need to respect the time of everyone who has already arrived. If you have the majority of the group, start off the meeting and the remaining participants can be brought up to speed later.

You can get everyone's attention by stating out loud "Let's get started" and then kick off the meeting. If people are deep in conversation and don't hear you the first time, call out politely but assertively "Can I get your attention? In the interest of time, I'd like to get the meeting started."

Welcome everyone as a group

Now that you have the group's attention and the meeting is officially kicked off, *welcome your participants* and thank them for attending. By simply stating "Welcome everyone, and thank you for coming today," you immediately start the meeting on a positive note. Don't miss out on an important, yet easy opportunity to make your participants feel welcomed and their attendance appreciated. They have likely prioritized your meeting over other activities to participate.

Hold introductions and capture attendance

There is significant value in asking your participants to introduce themselves and capturing their attendance. Ask everyone to go around the room physically or virtually by phone, video, etc. This has the following two purposes:

1.	This allows everyone to know who they are interacting with and what perspectives are at the meeting table
2.	This allows you to know who is present or absent from your expected participant list

- **Holding introductions:** Unless you are pulling together a group that already meets regularly (such as a staff or committee meeting), you are best to *assume that everyone doesn't already know each other*. People often converse with others by phone or email but never get the opportunity to put a face to a familiar name until they cross paths in a meeting.

  If you have new people on your team or various departments, groups or levels of the organization in the same room, go around the room to *allow for introductions*. Make sure you invite the people on the phone to identify who is present. When those on the phone introduce themselves, periodically two or more people may speak at once. Make sure you clarify who is on the line by asking them to repeat themselves and verify who you hear.

- **Capturing attendance**: *Track who attends* your meeting and who has sent their regrets (or in some cases, who doesn't show up). This is especially important in meetings where critical issues are discussed, and decisions are made.

  Keeping track of meeting participants through minutes provides a historical record of who participated in key discussions. If a decision is challenged at a later date, a *record of participants* could identify who provided input into that decision along with a record of the discussion.

If you have a small group around the table where you already know everyone, *self-track who is present* and write their names as they enter the room. If you have assigned the role of note-taker to someone else, be sensitive to whether or not they know everyone. Introductions will eliminate this risk.

Another option is to bring a *copy of the meeting invite list* and check the names off as they are called out. If it's a very large group, you can *read out the names* and ask them to identify if they are present.

There may be a benefit to having a *sign-in sheet* available. This can be passed around the room. However, do this in addition to the roundtable introductions. Use this method to collect any additional information such as their job title, organization, email or other contact information that might be relevant for future use.

One additional thing to take into consideration is if more than one person in the meeting has the same first name, use at least their last initial when capturing who was in attendance.

Lay out the meeting purpose, objectives and expected outcomes

Provide your participants with *context-setting* around the purpose of the meeting and what you hope to achieve. Your participants may have come from another meeting, phone call or another distraction that is still on their minds. Context setting resets their thinking and focuses them on the meeting's intent.

This should include:

• Why you have brought everyone to the table
• What your objectives are for the meeting
• What outcomes you expect to see by the end of the meeting
• What process the group will go through to accomplish the objectives and expected outcomes

By providing a *short, high-level overview*, this will help them transition their thoughts to the present conversation. This activity brings everyone on the same page and sets them up for the meeting discussion.

If you are holding a follow-up meeting to a previous discussion, give a brief overview of what happened the last time and the reason why everyone has come back to the table. This is especially important if time has lapsed since the initial meeting.

Review the meeting agenda

Walk the group through the discussion topics identified on the agenda. Depending on the purpose and length of your meeting, the number of agenda items will vary. This *lays out what the planned discussion will look like*. If it makes sense to do so, ask your participants if they have any additional agenda items they want to add.

Set clear expectations for the meeting

Finally, when you are wrapping up the opening activities of the meeting, let the group know if you have any specific expectations. This is where you would *provide any ground rules* for the discussion and ask for agreement. See if the group has any other ideas to share.

Each meeting is unique, and therefore the expectations you set will be situation-specific. Here is a preliminary list of expectations you can review and select from:

• Looking for everyone's active participation in the discussion
• Interested in hearing everyone's perspective
• This is meant to be a collaborative discussion
• We will watch the clock and make sure we end on time
• Be respectful of each other
• Don't talk over each other
• Be respectful of differing opinions
• Let everyone have the opportunity to present their point of view
• Be present and engaged
• Laptops and cell phones should be tucked away
• If you need to perform any non-meeting related activities, quietly step out of the room
• Today is a safe environment to express your opinions and ideas
• There are no bad ideas
• Ask questions while they are fresh in your mind
• Leave questions and comments to the end

Select any expectations that make sense for your meeting. Communicate these to the group and revisit them throughout the meeting if you find the group has veered from what was agreed upon.

Once you have completed these essential opening activities during the first few minutes of your meeting, start to delve into the agenda item topics and begin leading the meeting discussion.

Step 1	Step 2	Step 3
Before	*During*	*After*

Lead the Meeting Discussion

All meetings require someone *to lead the group through the discussion*. As the meeting lead, your responsibility is to make sure your participants are engaged in the conversation, stay on track, and contribute effectively to the identified agenda items.

After starting the meeting, you should have already done the following:

• Welcomed everyone
• Held introductions and captured attendance
• Laid out the meeting purpose, objectives and expected outcomes
• Reviewed the agenda
• Stated clear expectations

For the duration of the meeting, you will need to *pay special attention to a number of factors* that can help you achieve your expected outcomes. This chapter lays out a number of considerations for leading the meeting discussion.

What should be considered when leading the meeting discussion?

Active listening
Active listening is an important skill of a great meeting lead. *Listen carefully* to the information that each participant offers during the discussion. The following behaviors are associated with active listening:

• Concentrate on the words spoken and key messages
• Face the participant speaking
• Listen without passing judgment or jumping to conclusions
• Avoid interrupting or speaking over anyone
• Wait for an appropriate pause before asking clarifying questions
• Watch for non-verbal communication through body language and facial expressions
• Summarize the key messages to validate what you heard

Allocating meeting roles

Understanding your role, and clarifying the roles of others, are essential for an effective and productive meeting. These roles can include the following:

• Meeting lead
• Note-taker
• Scribe
• Time-keeper
• AV support
• Meeting participant

- **Meeting lead** - As the meeting lead, your overall role is to *make sure the meeting moves forward* successfully and achieves the expected outcomes. However, the meeting lead is broken down into *two sub-roles*. The first is the *chair role* and the second is the *facilitator role*. Often these are covered off by the same person. However, this is not always the case. There are situations where having two different individuals is beneficial.

  The *chair role* focuses on the *content* of what is discussed and does the following:

• Opens the meeting
• Reviews the agenda
• Provides context-setting
• Sets expectations

• Manages the discussion to the agenda items and keeps the group moving forward
• Wraps up the meeting by summarizing the key discussion points, decisions, action items, and next steps
• Thanks the meeting participants
• Closes the meeting

The *facilitator role* also keeps the group moving forward but focuses mostly on the *process* of how the content is discussed and does the following:

• Makes sure the meeting participants are engaged and collaborating
• Guides the group to keep the discussion on track
• Asks clarifying questions
• Captures the discussion points accurately
• Encourages active participation
• Determines what tools are used
• Identifies the methodology for how the discussion unfolds
• Defines how interactions are managed

A key element that distinguishes the two roles is *neutrality*. A chair *may have an opinion or expertise* that they choose to share in the meeting. However, a facilitator is there *as a neutral party* and does not exert their opinion. Instead, the facilitator draws the ideas, opinions, and expertise from others and uses that information to support the discussion.

• **Note-taker** - This role is responsible for capturing key discussions points, decisions, risks and issues, action items and next steps. This is done either electronically by *typing these items on a laptop* or by *transcribing them onto a notepad or notebook*. There are times where the meeting lead takes on this role and tracks the information while keeping the meeting going. It *takes experience to take both roles on* at once. The complexity of the discussion will help determine if someone else should take on this role.

Another individual is often tasked with note-taking for the *development of meeting minutes* (a historical record of the meeting). This individual should have a basic understanding of the content to make sure the notes are captured accurately. Consider the complexity of the discussion when identifying who would be appropriate to capture the conversation.

- **Scribe -** This role is similar to the note-taker except *documentation is done more visually* to allow your participants to see what is being captured. This is done at the front or around the room. Key points and action items are captured on flip charts, whiteboards, a computer screen projected in the room, sticky notes, etc. This is done by the meeting lead or tasked to another individual. In meetings where the participants break out into groups, a scribe could be identified within each group to track the discussion.

- **Time-keeper -** The time-keeper plays a key role in *managing the time*. This role will check in with the meeting lead periodically around the time left for an agenda item, and when the meeting is close to wrapping up. The time-keeper role is especially important if you have allocated specific times for each discussion or breakout group. This demonstrates to your participants that you respect their time by managing it effectively.

- **AV support -** This role makes sure that any *audiovisual needs of the meeting* are taken care of. This includes opening a teleconference line, setting up a projector, setting up or testing of any microphones in the room, etc. In many cases, the meeting lead will take on this role. You may want to assign this to someone who is *technologically savvy*. This role assists in mitigating any challenges that arise with the audiovisual equipment.

- **Meeting participant -** This role includes *all your meeting invitees* who are there as key stakeholders and subject matter experts. Just as the name suggests, these individuals are in the meeting to participate in the discussion, ask questions, provide answers, and offer their valuable expertise to the agenda item topics.

Asking your participants clarifying questions
One of your goals is to *draw out information from your participants* to support the meeting discussion. You can do this by *being inquisitive* during the conversation to gain further input, knowledge, and clarity around key points that arise. Asking simple questions such as "Could you tell me more about that?" or "Can you be more specific?" can help you tease out more information.

If a participant is *long-winded*, and you are trying to capture their key points, ask them to clarify by saying: "How can I articulate that in a sentence or two for the meeting notes?" or "What is the specific action item you want me to capture?" This forces that individual to reflect on what they just said, and reiterate it more succinctly. Another strategy is to repeat back what you heard in your own words and ask for validation.

Being flexible and staying calm
When leading meetings on a regular basis, you quickly learn that *unexpected circumstances* can occur at any time. There is an infinite number of challenges, but here are a few you might encounter:

• Your laptop screen turns blacks unexpectedly
• The teleconference line or call-in number isn't working
• The projector light begins blinking on and off during a presentation
• The flip chart markers in the room are dried out
• The meeting discussion starts to veer off-track

You can never plan for every possible situation. However, *you can always control how you react* when the unexpected arises. Challenges like these can easily result in your heart to start pounding, your body to start sweating and your mind to start racing. Despite any physical reaction, how you act on the exterior is what is important. If you *remain cool and calm*, your participants will maintain confidence in you regardless of challenges that are out of your control.

Capturing key information from the discussion
As the meeting discussion unfolds, it is important to accurately capture:

• Any key discussion points
• All decisions made by the group
• Any identified risks or issues
• All action items and who is responsible
• Any required next steps after the meeting

If you are not acting as the note-taker or scribe, it is still valuable to *self-capture the action items* discussed. This allows you to provide a *quick summary at the end* of the meeting of who is responsible for what actions.

Capturing this information will allow you to do the following after the meeting:

• Develop meeting minutes or action logs
• Implement key decisions made
• Mitigate any risks or issues discovered
• Follow up on action items
• Follow through on any identified next steps

If you find that during the discussion you are not 100% clear on either the decision, action item or next step, *pause the discussion and ask for clarity*. Repeat what you heard and ask questions including "Did I understand you correctly?" or "Did I capture this accurately?" This will allow the meeting details to be documented correctly and the necessary follow up to be done.

This consideration will be discussed in greater detail in the next chapter.

Completing time checks

Periodically throughout the meeting, it's a good idea to *check the time* to make sure the discussion is on-track. Announce a time check when the meeting is *coming up on 10 minutes* before the end. This signals to the group you are managing the time appropriately and honoring your promise to end the meeting without going over. Your participants will become aware that they should contribute any final thoughts, including action items and next steps.

If someone else has been assigned the role of time-keeper, request that they keep you informed on the amount of time left throughout the meeting.

Engaging your meeting participants

The *level of engagement* of your participants determines whether or not you will have a successful meeting. Maintaining their engagement includes encouraging participation, asking them key questions, and keeping the conversation moving through the agenda items.

When engaging the group, *capture all perspectives in the room*. Naturally, some participants will have more to contribute. However, your role is to make sure that everyone in the room has the opportunity to be heard, understood and to feel valued.

If you have participants joining by phone, *take the extra initiative to keep them engaged*. Since they are not in the room, you *cannot visually assess* their level of engagement. Check in frequently with those on the line, especially with agenda items that are relevant to them. Periodically, complete a sound check by asking the participants on the phone if they can hear the discussion in the room. If needed, *repeat any key points or questions*. Invite the group in the room to be mindful that those on the phone may be challenged in hearing the conversation.

Managing challenging discussions

Meeting discussions can *unexpectedly take a turn* and become challenging to manage. As the meeting lead, it's your role to facilitate the group through the discussion and *take control when conflict arises*. A difficult meeting conversation can be triggered when the following situations occur:

• Participants feel they are not being heard or understood
• There are differing opinions
• There is a high emotional connection with an agenda topic
• Personalities dominate the conversation
• Participants perceive that they have something to lose

While it's not always possible to be fully prepared for when this might happen, there are a few things you can do to keep the group on track and productive. These include the following:

- **Create a safe environment -** If you anticipate in advance that the meeting might be *contentious or highly emotional*, set the expectation at the beginning of the meeting that this is a safe environment for the discussion and encourage all participants to offer their opinions and insights.

  If you are not expecting the discussion to take a sudden, unexpected turn, *take control of the meeting* by stating clearly that this is meant to be a safe, open discussion. Ask your participants to each provide their input without interruptions. Request that everyone *acts respectfully and remains open-minded* to any different, yet valuable perspectives in the room.

- **Remain respectful and positive -** The group will *feed off the energy and presence of others* in the room. As the lead, it's important that you *model the appropriate behaviors*. Manage your own language, tone, and body language to make sure you are perceived as being calm, respectful, open and positive. Take a deep breath and monitor your own emotions to allow yourself to focus solely on helping the group resolve the identified issues.

- **Acknowledge the challenges -** Once you identify that a difficult discussion has surfaced, it's important to *immediately acknowledge with the group* that you recognize that an issue or challenge is present. If you attempt to ignore the issue that has been addressed or try to change the topic, it will *inevitably resurface* and result in further tensions and strained relationships.

  Regardless of whether the challenge should be discussed at this time or set aside for later, you should, at the very least, let the group know that you recognize the issue has been raised.

- **Focus on the issue at hand -** When *emotions begin to run high*, you may come across situations where participants *resort to blaming behaviors* when they are dissatisfied with a process, outcome, or conflicting personality.

Your role as the meeting lead is to *quickly de-escalate the conversation* by restating and summarizing the issue at hand. Rephrase the discussion points to *clearly state the specific problem* and remove the focus from any specific individual or group.

- **Get to the root of the challenge** – It's important to gain an understanding of the *underlying reason* when a difficult discussion arises. You can begin to delve into the root of the challenge by asking your participants open-ended, clarifying questions to gain a better understanding of the issue. Ask your participants to "Tell me more about that" to encourage them to explain further.

  Your role is to make sure that *more than one perspective is heard* at the table. If you find one participant dominating the discussion, reflect back to that individual what you heard to acknowledge their key points and then state "I'd like to get some thoughts and input from others in the group."

- **Take conversations offline** - Not all challenging discussions should be addressed as a larger group. You may want to inform your participants that the *conversation will be taken offline.* Consider this option if you have concerns that:

• The issue will completely sidetrack and interrupt the meeting
• There are significant behavioral issues to address
• The conversation has a private nature that shouldn't be discussed as a group

Inform the group that you are placing the offline discussion on the list of action items. Then, *quickly bring the group back to the agenda* and intended discussion.

Managing to the agenda

Since the agenda provides the *roadmap* for the meeting, you should revisit it regularly during the discussion. Use this supportive tool *to keep the conversation on track*. Throughout the meeting, check to see what agenda items you completed and what topics remain.

Keep the group moving by indicating you need to bring the current agenda item to a close. Wrap up the topic by asking if there are any key decisions, action items, and next steps related to that agenda item.

If you allocated times to each item in advance, this would give you an additional tool to *track the meeting's progress* and keep the discussion moving at an appropriate pace.

Minimizing the use of industry "jargon" and acronyms

Every industry, organization, and department will *naturally develop their own, unique "language"* of specialized terminology and acronyms that are related to their body of work. For example, common terms and phrases are completely different in each industry, such as banking, health care, legal and construction.

Meetings bring various participants together. It's common to forget that when using your own, specialized words or expressions, others may not understand. This is often referred to as *"jargon."* You can quickly form a *communication barrier* unless you level set at the beginning of the meeting what terms and acronyms you will be using, or as they arise in the discussion.

This also applies to the notes and meeting minutes that are developed. Capture key discussion points, action items and next steps *with the reader in mind*. Always use the assumption that the reader is unfamiliar with the group's terminology and acronyms. An example is when a new team member joins and reviews previous meeting minutes to catch up. If the document is full of acronyms without a description somewhere, then the minutes did not serve the purpose for which they were intended.

Monitoring your own facial expressions and body language
As the meeting lead, *pay attention to your own facial expressions and body language* during the meeting. This is especially true in times where the conversation is challenging, and differing opinions occur. Your own body language can *set the tone* for the rest of the group. Here are some tips to be mindful of when leading the discussion:

- **Maintain warm or neutral facial expressions** - Your expressions can instantly tell the group how you feel about the discussion. When the meeting is going well, or you are encouraging a participant to be engaged, *a warm smile can go a long way*. However, when a discussion becomes challenging, and emotions begin to run high, it's necessary to *maintain a cool, calm exterior* which includes keeping facial expressions neutral. If not, a facial expression that is interpreted as disapproval, disappointment or disagreement can quickly cause the conversation to break down further.

- **Face the group** - Try to *keep your body facing the participants* in the room. When you turn away from the group, this closes your body language off, and it becomes more difficult to communicate. This can occur when scribing information on flip charts or viewing a presentation on a screen. Always position yourself in a way that you can still face the room, even if you are at a slight angle. Consider the space setup to help minimize turning your back to the group.

- **Maintain eye contact** - Your eye contact should be friendly and encouraging. If someone hasn't spoken up, a friendly glance in their direction might prompt them to offer a suggestion. By *keeping your eyes focused on your participants* and less on a screen, laptop, notepad, etc., this allows the group to feel you are actively listening and engaging them.

- **Keep your body language open** - Pay attention to the signals your body sends *by how you position and posture yourself*. Standing or sitting with your arms crossed sends a negative message and could be misinterpreted as anger, disapproval or disagreement. Keeping your arms rested gently to your sides, or on the table in front of you sends a more positive, open message to the group.

Maintain a *relaxed posture* when you are leading the meeting. You can also lean in slightly when you are listening or addressing any of your participants.

- **Minimize multi-tasking** - There are times when multi-tasking is necessary during the meeting. For example, you may be leading the discussion while bringing up the next presentation, and scribing the key discussion points on flip chart paper. To some extent, this is normal. However, try to *limit unnecessary multi-tasking* such as checking your own emails or glancing at your phone. You might be giving the impression you are not paying attention and have more important things to do.

Monitoring your participants' facial expressions and body language
People will naturally react (either positively, neutrally or negatively) to information and conversations in a meeting. They will often *unknowingly display their feelings* through their facial expressions and body language. As the meeting lead, you can *use this non-verbal communication* to determine if you should continue engaging your participants in the same manner or change your approach.

- **Positive facial expressions and body language** - There are several, positive behaviors and reactions that indicate your participants are *well-engaged* in the discussion. These could include the following:

• Good eye contact with you and other participants in the room
• Leaning forward and visibly listening to the discussion
• Head movements such as nodding in agreement
• Smiling or neutral facial expressions
• Open body postures and hand gestures

- **Negative facial expressions and body language** - Watch for negative facial expressions and behaviors to determine when participants are *disengaged or displaying behaviors* that may need to be addressed.

• Eye rolling or avoiding eye contact
• Focusing attention on non-meeting related activities including using cell phones, tablets, laptops, etc.
• Closed body postures including crossed arms and legs, slouching and leaning away from the discussion
• Finger tapping on the table or foot tapping on the floor
• Facial expressions indicating confusion or disagreement

Your participants will *provide you with a great deal of information non-verbally* about how engaged they are, and how they feel about the content. Closely monitor these cues. Reach out and say "How are you feeling about this?" or "What questions or concerns do you have?"

If you recognize body language that indicates a participant is disengaged or disagrees but isn't openly challenging what they heard, *take the extra effort to engage that individual.* Ask that participant if anything is missing from their perspective to help re-engage them into the discussion. You can say: "(Insert name), I would like to hear your perspective. Does this reflect your thinking? Are we missing anything here?"

Pausing for group feedback, input, and questions
Throughout the course of the meeting, look for moments that make sense to *pause the conversation.* Ask your participants if they have questions or feedback. After each agenda item is an ideal time to pause and invite the group to add their thoughts or ask for clarity.

Watch for other moments during the discussion that makes sense to take a pause. If you *begin to notice body language or facial expressions* that indicate confusion, or an eagerness to provide input, say "Let's pause here for a moment. Are there any questions or comments from the group?"

Preventing the discussion from being side-tracked
Meeting discussions can easily become side-tracked. This is often a result of:

• A participant stating a personal opinion
• A participant raising an irrelevant point
• Poor facilitation by the meeting lead

This always happens innocently at first. However, the *discussion can take on a life of its own* once others start to weigh in. This could result in the *agenda being lost* and a second, follow up meeting being booked to discuss the same topic from the original discussion. How the meeting lead handles the situation and brings the conversation back on track is an example of what sets an effective and ineffective meeting apart.

Recognize if the side-tracked discussion needs to be taken offline for further exploration or if it needs to end.

If further discussion is needed, be assertive, jump in, and state "This sounds like an important conversation. We should explore this further, but this is not part of our agenda today." Let the group know you are capturing the conversation as an action item and assign someone to take the lead. If you are capturing action items visually, write this on the whiteboard, flip chart, etc.

If the conversation does not need to continue, tell the group "It sounds like we are getting a little off-track. We have more items on the agenda that we still need to get to today. Let's refocus the discussion." Redirect the participants back to the original agenda and if needed, remind the group what the discussion was before it moved off-topic.

Referring to a Terms of Reference, if needed
If your meeting is related to an ongoing committee, you may have a document that was developed when the committee began called a "Terms of Reference." This document describes:

• The purpose of the committee
• What the group has set out to achieve
• How they will manage their meetings
• Whether they have decision-making authority
• The roles and responsibilities of the committee
• The committee membership

You may come across moments during your meeting when it would be beneficial to revisit the Terms of Reference. Consider this when you feel that:

• Decisions are being made that the committee does not have authority over
• The meeting conversation regularly veers off-topic
• The role of the committee is unclear around an agenda topic
• A difficult decision is needed, and the group is unsure of the committee decision-making process (consensus, consultative, majority voting, etc.)

Supporting effective decision-making

A *variety of decisions are made during meetings.* Some arise naturally throughout the discussion while others are pre-planned as agenda items. These can vary in size from small and operational, to large and strategic decisions that have significant impacts on an organization.

To support decision-making, it is important to know the following:

• What decision needs to be made
• The purpose of the decision
• The different types of decision-making
• How the decision will be handled by the group
• The criteria that will be used to support the decision
• The process for decision-making

- **What decision needs to be made?** If a *decision is previously identified and placed on an agenda*, then the details should already be fairly clear. Typically, reserving space on an agenda is for larger decisions requiring discussion and input from others. When this happens, a mutual understanding of the decision needed should be easy to develop because it has already been pre-planned for the meeting. Ideally, a description of the decision should be created in advance and either pre-circulated, brought forward at the meeting verbally or documented, or placed on a presentation slide for the group to review.

However, as agenda items are discussed, *other decisions may arise from the conversation*. These tend to be more operational in nature and are not typically pre-defined before the meeting.

- **What is the purpose of the decision?** The purpose of the decision describes "why" the decision is needed. Ask yourself or the group if the reason a decision is needed is to allow you to move forward, mitigate a risk, make a larger decision, etc.

  Decisions are often brought forward at meetings as a means of collecting input, discussing, consulting and formulating an appropriate choice. Take into consideration how important the decision is, why it is required, and what is the consequence of not deciding.

- **What are the different types of decision-making?** There are several ways that decisions can be made. Here is an overview of the common decision-making styles used in meetings:

1. **Directive:** Some decisions *fall under the accountability of one participant* in the room. A directive style of decision-making is when the owner of the decision decides based on the information they have access to, at the time. They don't seek input or feedback from others. This is an independent style, and the rest of the group may be expected to respond by implementing the decision as needed. Leaders who have full authority over their area may choose to use this decision-making style to make operational decisions.

2. **Consultative:** Like the directive style, this approach has *one participant with the authority* to make the decision. However, what is unique is the decision-maker *seeks out input, feedback and recommendations* from others. This input is used to inform the decision, but ultimately, this individual still has the final say. Larger, strategic decisions will often be made using this approach.

3. **Majority Voting:** This approach provides the opportunity for *multiple participants to weigh in* on a decision. Everyone in the room may or may not have an equal vote depending on who the

decision will impact and their role in the meeting. For those that are voting, at least 51% of the vote is needed in one direction or another for a decision to be final. Committees will often use this approach when multiple people are needed to weigh in on a decision.

4. **Consensus-based:** Consensus-based decision-making is the most challenging to achieve but is powerful when it is accomplished. This seeks to *gain agreement by all participants* who have a say on the decision. To achieve consensus, 100% of the participants need to agree on the same decision. This is used when buy-in from everyone is needed to sustain the results.

- **Determine how the group will handle the decision** - If the decision is pre-planned as an agenda item, determine what decision-making style is needed based on the participants in the room, the level of authority they have and the impact the decision will have on others. If the decision arises unexpectedly, determine if the group understands who the decision-makers are. If this can't be identified right away, place this as an action item for immediate, off-line discussion.

- **Develop criteria to support the decision** - Each decision is unique and will *require its own set of criteria* to support the group to make the right selection. This might be a list of considerations or a decision-making tree that says "if A occurs, we should choose 1, and if B occurs, we should choose 2." If the need for a decision is pre-planned before the meeting, it might be helpful to have a set of criteria developed in advance. Otherwise, open the discussion during the meeting to see what criteria should be used to weigh the decision against.

Some examples of *decision-making criteria* include:

• **Alignment** – does one decision align better with your organization's goals over another?
• **Risks** – is there a greater risk associated with any of the decision choices?
• **Resources** – are there different resource implications depending on the decision?

• **Priority** - are there some activities that should be prioritized ahead of others that might affect the decision?
• **Return on Investment** – is one decision over another going to result in better returns?
• **Ease of Implementation** – Will one decision be easier to implement than another?

The decision-making criteria you use should be directly related to the decision you are trying to make.

- **Define the decision-making process** - Use a standard process when making decisions that include the following steps:

• Define the problem and **identify the decision** required
• **Gather information** about the options. Ask open-ended questions and discuss alternatives. Determine who can offer insights and new ideas. Think about what the impacts are because of the decision. Identify what data is available to support the decision
• Develop a set of **criteria** to support the decision-making
• Identify who has **decision-making authority** (one owner vs. the whole group)
• Review and weigh the available decision-making **options**
• **Select** from the available options

Some decisions require input from a variety of people and can take time. Others can be made quickly. Every decision will always be unique, but these steps outlined above are appropriate regardless of whether the decision is large or small.

Supporting participants on the phone
Although many of the same considerations exist for any meeting format, there are a few additional elements that are unique when participants are joining by phone.

- **Circulate the agenda in advance** – It's always good practice to *circulate the agenda prior to the meeting* regardless of whether the meeting is by phone. This is especially true since you can't physically hand out an agenda. By providing the agenda in advance, this allows your participants to follow along throughout the meeting.

- **Log in a few minutes early** - *Log into the teleconference line at least a few minutes early.* This gives you the extra time to check to see if it's working correctly and to troubleshoot any challenges.

- **Track attendance accurately** - Track everyone who joins the call. *Collect names* as people start to join the line. Then verify who is on the line once the meeting begins to make sure you have captured everyone. This also allows everyone on the line to know who is participating since they can't physically see the other participants.

  One challenge that may occur is several people introduce themselves at once making it unclear who has joined. Pause and take a moment to *clarify who is present* by stating the names you captured and ask if anyone has been missed. If you have an extra-large group, read out the list of invitees instead and ask each participant to identify if they are present. Then, ask if you missed anyone in case the meeting was delegated.

- **Ask participants on the phone to mute** - Often your participants are unaware that their surroundings may result in background noise that can be distracting to everyone on the call. Ask those on the phone *to mute while listening* to the conversation.

  Ask them to mute their phone also if they need to step away for a few minutes and to *not place the call on hold*. They may be unaware that their organization's phone system plays music or advertising when a call is held. This is distracting and will ultimately grind your meeting to a halt until they return.

- **Communicate page numbers or locations in documents under review** - If documents were circulated prior to the meeting with the intent of reviewing it during the call, make sure you clearly *communicate what file you have open and the page or slide number.* Meeting participants not located in the room lack any visual cues to turn a page or move to the next slide. Additional communication is needed to allow everyone to follow along.

- **Give participants time to respond** - Remember, if you ask for input from someone on the line, they need a few seconds to unmute before contributing to the conversation. However, if some time goes by where they have not responded, a quick reminder that they may still be muted is helpful as they may be responding without realizing.

- **Pause and invite questions and feedback** - Remember, visual cues are absent making it challenging to know if the group has questions or feedback. Make sure you pause regularly and *ask if anyone has anything to add*. You can also invite the group to jump in at any time with questions or feedback.

- **Take the extra time to engage everyone on the phone** - Certain agenda items may be more relevant to specific participants on the line. If the discussion continues and those individuals have not contributed, *ask them directly for their perspective*. Let them know you value their feedback. As you go through the conversation, invite everyone to offer their thoughts on each agenda topic.

As you can see, there are many considerations when leading a group through a meeting discussion. Allow this chapter to help you be more mindful of the additional needs and complexities that come with chairing and facilitating meetings. By embracing these concepts, you will demonstrate and prove yourself to be an effective and valuable meeting lead.

Chapter 16

Step 1 *Before* > Step 2 *During* > Step 3 *After*

Capture and Document the Meeting Discussion

If a meeting discussion isn't documented, it might as well have never happened. It soon becomes a *distant memory* with participants trying to remember what was said and what was agreed upon. Without any information to fall back on, this could *escalate into additional, unnecessary meetings* to rediscuss the original agenda topics.

However, if a meeting is well-documented, there is a *solid, historical record* that outlines the discussion and any decisions made. This provides a record of the conversation for not only your organization but also for yourself to reference at any time.

This chapter explores what information should be tracked from the discussion, the importance of documenting this, and who should be doing this activity.

What information from the meeting discussion should be documented?

There are several, important elements of the discussion that are valuable to track throughout the meeting. These include the following:

• Key discussion points for each agenda item
• Any decisions that are made
• Risks or issues brought forward, with any mitigating strategies
• Action items for follow up, with who is responsible, and expected timeframes

These elements are described in further detail below.

Key discussion points

A key discussion point is a *brief statement that summarizes an important detail of a meeting discussion*. At least two to three key points should be documented for each agenda item. These provide a high-level summary of what was discussed.

Use your judgment to determine if you need to track more or less information, depending on:

• The complexity of the discussion
• The length of the discussion
• The formality of the meeting
• The expectations around how detailed the meeting minutes should be

Capture enough information to be able to go back to the summarized key points, and have a solid understanding of what was discussed and the outcomes achieved.

Some *tips for capturing the key discussion points* include:

• Remain neutral
• Keep the discussion points objective
• Capture the points in the spirit of which they are intended (don't add your own impressions or viewpoints)
• Paraphrasing (re-wording) is ok, but don't change the meaning
• Ask the group to repeat a key point, if clarity is needed
• Practice active listening to identify what information is relevant
• If note-taking by hand, consider creating your own shorthand of acronyms and symbols to allow you to document the details faster

Decisions

When capturing a decision, you are documenting the *conclusion or resolution to a problem, challenge or question*. Regardless of how large or small a decision, it should be documented. *Implementation and enforcement* become significantly easier if it's recorded.

Depending on the *decision-making style used* (directive, consultative, majority voting or consensus-based), it may be beneficial to track which style was used, and the decision-makers involved.

Risks and issues

A risk is an *uncertain potential for something to happen* that is usually unwanted, and could have a negative impact on an individual, team, process, project, organization, etc. An issue is when the *potential challenge has become a reality*, and is already happening now.

As the agenda topics are discussed, risks or issues may arise during the conversation. Document these along with any strategies to either mitigate them, or improve the situation.

Should a risk be realized, there is now a record of it being discussed, along with any identified next steps to manage it. For issues, the next steps to resolve the challenge can be referenced, and acted upon immediately.

If a risk management plan is required, you can easily reference the meeting documentation for this information.

Here are some examples of risks and issues that might be captured during a meeting:

Example 1:

> *Risk: With the upcoming retirements, we might be short-staffed if we are unable to fill the positions right away.*
>
> *Issue: With the recent retirements, and the lack of specialized talent in the area to draw from, we are now short-staffed.*

Example 2:

> *Risk: If we are unable to balance the budget by the end of the month, we will need to look at what program to eliminate.*
>
> *Issue: The budget was not balanced, and our expenses have already reached our annual amount. A decision must be made on which program to close immediately to balance the budget.*

Action items

An action item is any *follow up task or activity* that has been identified during a discussion where *someone is required to do something within a certain timeframe*. Most meetings will have at least a short list of action items generated by the end of the discussion.

It often takes *active listening to recognize* when an action item arises. There are times when the action item is very clear. Someone may state "I'm going to follow up with…" or "After this meeting, we should do…". However, action items are not always that easy to spot. The key is being able to distinguish an action item from the general conversation.

When listening to the discussion, *pay attention to action-oriented phrases* during the meeting and use this as a guide to help identify action items as they arise:

• "I'm/We're going to have to…"
• "I/We need to talk to…"
• "I/We should look at…"
• "I/We need to bring this to…"

You may find there are times you need to tease out what action items there are from the discussion. After each agenda topic comes to an end, *ask the group what follow up is needed*.

- **Be specific** - The more specific you can make the action items, the better. This provides *greater role clarity* for your participants. Document the actions required, along with who is responsible, and the expected timeframe for completion. Tracking action items is a necessity, or else you lose the ability to follow up, and hold the owners accountable.

- **Ongoing action items** - Periodically you may capture actions items that are *ongoing with no specific completion date* identified. This is acceptable and simply needs to be documented for continued reference.

- **Future-oriented action items** - Future-oriented action items may also arise that are *not required to be addressed immediately*. By capturing this information, it allows you and your participants to reference and re-visit the action item down the road.

- **Equally responsible action items** - When you identify an action item that *everyone in the room is equally responsible for*, this will require extra effort on your part to hold the whole group accountable. This is where *tracking attendance adds additional value* because you now have a record of who is there, and who you need to follow up with if any regrets were given.

Here is a sample list of action items to give you an idea of what information should be captured:

Natalie will take the identified questions and develop an online survey to collect customer experience feedback. This will be distributed by next Monday.

Adam will draft the process map of our new workflow and circulate this to the team by Friday.

Logan will develop the project's communication plan using the template discussed, and present this document at the next project team meeting.

Susanna will pull a sub-group together to develop the financial report for the past quarter, and circulate this to the Financial Operations Committee by the end of next week.

Michelle will contact the three potential vendors this week, and schedule the vendor demo presentations before the end of the month.

These examples demonstrate who is responsible, the specific action required, and when it will be completed by.

Why is it important to document the meeting discussion?

There are a variety of reasons why it's important to document the meeting discussion. These include:

• Providing a **historical record** of the discussion
• Allowing the ability to **hold others accountable** for their action items
• Supporting the **implementation of decisions** made
• Allowing the discussion to be **shared** more broadly
• Providing a resource for **future reference**
• Providing the content to **develop meeting minutes and action logs**
• Providing the content to **develop a follow-up meeting communication**

Who should capture and document the meeting discussion?

The meeting lead holds the responsibility of documenting the meeting. You may choose to take on this role yourself. However, you also have the option to delegate the role of *note-taker* or *scribe* to someone else in attendance.

If someone else is capturing the discussion, make sure they understand *what information is relevant to track*. Depending on the complexity of the discussion, periodically say "I think that's an important point we should document." Ask the note-taker or scribe to track the information. Reiterate the key point to make sure it's documented effectively. This minimizes the risk of capturing less relevant information.

By tracking the key discussion points, risks and issues, decisions, and action items raised, you will have a *well-documented meeting*.

| Step 1 *Before* | Step 2 *During* | Step 3 *After* |

Close the Meeting

As the discussion wraps up, there are several activities you should do *to successfully close your meeting.* By this time, you have spent a considerable amount of energy leading the meeting and guiding the group through the agenda. Next, bring the discussion to a close while providing your participants with a clear understanding of any decisions made, action items, next steps and post-meeting expectations.

This chapter will walk you through the steps to close a meeting and any important considerations for this activity.

What steps are required to close out a meeting?

Here are the activities you should follow to wrap up the discussion:

• Provide a high-level overview of the key discussion points
• Review the identified action items
• Define any next steps
• Set any post-meeting expectations
• Evaluate the meeting in real-time, and capture any lessons learned
• Ask the group if they have any last questions or comments
• Thank your participants for their attendance and engagement
• Close out the meeting

These activities should *only take a few minutes* in total but are essential to closing the discussion effectively. Each of these steps are outlined in further detail below.

Provide a high-level overview of the discussion

As you start to wrap up the meeting, highlight any important discussion points, decisions made, and risks or issues with mitigating strategies that were discussed. *Sum this up in a few sentences*. If this is a longer meeting, such as a half or full day, you may require a few minutes or more to highlight the key points.

Review the identified action items

Review the action items captured, who is responsible, and when each action item should be completed by. *Validate this list* with the group and ask if you missed anything.

Define any next steps

Near the end of your meeting, *ask what next steps are required*. Your next steps are different from your action items in that they tend to be more process-related.

The next steps identify what happens once the meeting ends. These may include:

• Implementing any decisions made
• Defining how agenda items not discussed will be handled
• Holding any identified offline discussions
• Setting up any follow-up meetings as needed
• Circulating a follow-up communication
• Sending out any documents discussed at the meeting
• Following up with anyone who could not attend
• Developing the meeting minutes, summary or action log

Set any post-meeting expectations

Lay out any post-meeting expectations you have of your participants. Some examples include:

• Keep the meeting discussion confidential (for now, or permanently)
• Share any specific, key messages with colleagues, staff, teams, etc.

• Watch your email for a follow-up communication or further details
• Watch your email for further meeting appointments
• Complete all action items by the end of the week, month, before the next meeting, etc.
• Bring completed work, documents, research, etc. to the next meeting
• Circulate any feedback to the meeting lead only, the whole group, others, etc.

If the information discussed at the meeting should be shared, provide the group with *key, takeaway messages*. Often, participants never think to share the information beyond the walls of the meeting or fail to see how the content could be relevant to others. If this is an expectation, clearly communicate that the group should pass this along.

If the discussion should *remain confidential*, never assume your participants are aware of this, despite how obvious you feel this to be. This must be *clearly stated*. This is also true if developing a document that isn't ready for circulation beyond the participants. Set these expectations upfront before the meeting ends, or you may encounter challenges later.

Evaluate the meeting and capture any lessons learned
Every meeting is a *new learning opportunity*. Since each meeting is unique with different participants, agenda items, discussions, room layouts, meeting formats, etc., there will always be a *new experience to draw from*. As the meeting lead, you will experience the meeting with one perspective, and your participants will experience it from another perspective.

Invite *real-time feedback* from the group through a *quick check-in*. Inform the group, that in the interest of continuous improvement, you would like to invite them to offer any thoughts on the meeting.

Ask them what worked well, what didn't work so well, and what could be done differently at future meetings. Build this brief check-in into your meeting closeout to gain any *valuable insights* and real-time feedback. Remember, even *constructive feedback is positive*.

Once ideas are shared, thank everyone for their input and commit to applying any lessons learned to future meetings.

Should you run out of time and find yourself unable to collect feedback, you can invite the group to *offer input by email* after the meeting. However, in-the-moment feedback is always most helpful while it remains fresh in their minds.

Ask the group for any last questions or comments

With the meeting winding down, provide one last opportunity for your participants to *ask any questions* or to *offer any last thoughts*. You can simply ask the group "Are there any final questions or comments before we wrap up?".

Thank your participants

Thank your participants for their *attendance and active engagement* during the meeting. If you have people in the room and others on the phone, make sure you remember to thank everyone for joining.

Close the meeting

Your final step is to *officially end the meeting,* and let everyone know the meeting is over. This gives them a clear signal they are free to get up and leave. Indicate this to those on the phone, as well. Since these participants are not physically present, they *lack any visual cues* of people closing their notebooks or laptops, collecting their items, and getting up. They are commonly forgotten about, and meetings sometimes end without them being aware. This is especially true if the group breaks out immediately into post-meeting conversation, and the individuals on the phone are unsure if they need to stay on the line or disconnect.

Don't forget the importance of *ending the meeting on time*. Too often, meetings drag on well past the expected end time. As the meeting lead, it's your responsibility to prevent the group from going over. Meetings that run late prevent your participants from getting to other meetings on time, or from getting other work complete.

If your participants want to stay around after the meeting has ended to socialize, this is up to them. However, you want to effectively close the meeting to allow those who need to leave to do so.

How much time should be provided to close the meeting?

When you developed your agenda, you should have *allocated dedicated time* at the end of your meeting to properly close out the discussion. The amount of time you need is unique to each meeting, but you can estimate how long based on the following considerations:

The length of the meeting
Shorter meetings require less time to wrap up the discussion. If your meeting is scheduled for two hours or less, leave the last 10 minutes, or so, to close out. If you have an all-day session, consider dedicating the last half hour to this activity.

The complexity of the discussion
The amount of time you need to wrap up the discussion could be impacted by the complexity of your agenda. The higher the complexity, the more time you might need to properly wrap up the discussion.

The number of action items and next steps
If you identify a long list of action items and next steps during the meeting than expected, consider starting the close out a few minutes earlier to provide extra time to review these. This makes sure your participants are clear on their accountabilities and sets the right expectations for after the meeting.

If you are holding an in-person meeting, don't forget to leave the meeting room the way you found it. Turn off projectors and monitors, place tables and chairs the way you found them, clean up leftover handouts, and food and drinks, and turn off the lights and AV equipment.

Take the time to properly close out your meeting. This makes sure your participants leave with a clear understanding of decisions made, action items, next steps and post-meeting expectations. Your hard work will then be successfully transitioned to the follow-up activities needed in **Step 3: After the Meeting**.

Step 3: *After* the Meeting

Chapter 18

Step 1
Before

Step 2
During

Step 3
After

Develop Your Meeting Minutes or Action Log

During the meeting, you captured and documented key discussion points, decisions, risks and issues, and identified action items. Now, it's essential that you *transfer and translate this valuable information* into a format that can be referenced when needed in the future. This is typically done in one of two formats, including *meeting minutes or action logs.*

In this chapter, you will learn about the importance of meeting minutes and action logs, what information is typically captured in each of these formats, who is responsible for developing these documents, and what to do with them once they are created.

What are meeting minutes?

Many organizations use meeting minutes to capture the details of a discussion. Meeting minutes are documents that provide a *historical record of a meeting discussion, and include key discussion points for each agenda item, decisions made, risks or issues brought forward, with any mitigating strategies, and action items for follow up.*

The name "meeting minutes" *can be a little deceiving* as it may seem overwhelming to think about tracking a discussion *minute by minute.* However, this is generally not the case. Meeting minutes are documents that *provide a summary of what was discussed, agreed upon and identified as next steps.*

This document is created after a meeting takes place using the information captured during the discussion. Meeting minutes can vary in the amount of detail, depending on the type of meeting, and the expectations around tracking the conversation.

Why are meeting minutes important?

Meeting minutes are valuable as they offer you and your organization the ability to track decisions, hold others accountable, and provide you with a resource for future reference.

This document provides a record of:

• Key discussion points
• The evolution of ideas
• Issues, risks, and challenges that are raised
• Decisions made, the discussions leading up to the decisions, and when consensus is reached or not
• Who is accountable for each action item

What is the difference between formal and informal meeting minutes?

Meeting minutes can range from *very informal* where a few, key bullet points are captured highlighting the main discussion, to *very formal*, where a detailed description of the discussion is documented. Formal meeting minutes often include the names of everyone who contributed to each key discussion point.

The formality depends on the needs and expectations of your meeting. Formal committees, and meetings with executives and other senior leadership, often require formal meeting minutes. If you are ever unsure about how formal your meeting minutes should be, it's always best to *lean on the side of more formal*.

Formal meetings require proper record-keeping, especially if there are accountabilities to a larger body, such as another committee, government office, funding agency, etc.

Staff and team meetings are examples of less formal meetings. These will have more informal meeting minutes. Focus on high-level, key discussion points.

What should be included in meeting minutes?

When developing meeting minutes, there are several elements that should always be present. These include:

The name of the meeting
Add the name of your meeting to the *top of your document* for easy reference. If this is an ongoing meeting, such as a committee, the name will stay the same. Use the date and time to differentiate it from other meetings.

The date, time and location of the meeting
Capture the *logistics* of the meeting and place this under the meeting name. This is helpful in the future to make sure you are *referencing the correct document*.

The participants in attendance
During the meeting, you tracked the attendance, and any regrets or guests. List the *names* of who participated in your meeting.

Key discussion points for each agenda item
Include at least a few discussion points for each agenda item. These should provide a *high-level summary* of what was discussed. For more formal minutes, consider identifying the names of who contributed to each point. Capture this information objectively, and don't add your own personal thoughts to the document.

Decisions made
If decisions were made, include these in the meeting minutes. It's beneficial to identify the *decision-making style* used (directive, consultative, majority voting, or consensus-based) and *who* supported the decision.

Risks and issues raised
Make sure risks or issues that are discussed, along with any mitigating strategies, are well-documented. Include any next steps identified to *avoid or resolve* these.

Identified action items

List all identified action items for each agenda item, who is responsible for each one, and when they are expected to be completed by.

Figure 18.1: Meeting Minutes Example

Financial Management Software RFP Steering Committee
May 10, 2018 - 3:00 to 4:00 pm
Conference Room B

Attendees: Jayden Khoury, Ava Zhou, Susanna Peaton, Peter Romano, Jordan Daniels, Michele Rossi
Regrets: None

MEETING MINUTES

Welcome and Meeting Overview
- Susanna opened the meeting and attendance was captured.

- The steering committee reviewed the project scope that includes the identification, planning, and implementation of an industry-standard software system to meet our needs.

- This group came back together to review the project's current state and to discuss the preferred vendor recommendation made by the project team.

Project Updates
- The first round of evaluations by the project team narrowed down six vendor proposals to three.

- Vendor demos were completed on April 30th and the evaluation identified a clear front-runner from both a functionality and cost perspective.

- Reference checks were completed for all three vendors.

Recommendation
- The project team's recommendation to the steering committee was to move forward with Green Trail Financial.

- *Risk Identified:* Based on reference checks, additional time should be built into the implementation due to expected challenges with the data conversion.

- *Decision:* The steering committee reached consensus that Green Trail Financial would be the selected vendor. This will **remain confidential** until a contract is signed.

- *Action Item:* Susanna will reach out immediately to the legal team to begin the contract development.

- *Action Item:* Peter will track down our existing contract to see our current spend and contract termination requirements by next Friday, May 18.

What is an action log?

An action log is *one central location where all action items for a specific team, project or initiative, are captured and tracked over time*. This can be done in either an electronic or paper format.

An action log is *ideal for ongoing meetings*, such as staff or team meetings, planning or working groups, etc.

Why are action logs important?

When bringing participants together regularly to move your business activities forward, the number of follow up action items from these meetings *can quickly add up*. Tracking these action items and making sure that everyone is held accountable to completing them is a key success factor in any organization.

Action logs allow you to avoid losing sight of any follow-up activities, and is a useful tool for everyone to be *held accountable in a very visual way*.

Anyone can see the action items documented over time, along with the status of each. Information is tracked using a log instead of meeting minutes. This is valuable when all you need to manage is who is going to do what, and by when.

What should be included in an action log?

An action log includes several, important elements that are valuable to track. These include the following:

Action Item
State the action items with *as much detail as possible*. Lay out what follow-up tasks or activities need to happen.

Most Responsible Person
Identify who is responsible for following up on the action item. Even if there is an entire team that needs to move it forward, *identify one key individual* who will be responsible for making sure everyone follows through.

Date Identified

List the date the action item was originally identified. This will likely be the meeting date when the action item was *first discussed*.

Status

Here you can identify if the action item is *complete, in progress or not started*.

Date Completed

Once the action item is *moved to a complete status*, document the completion date here.

Comments/Notes

This section is filled out as needed. Use this as a place where *progress updates* about the action items are tracked. If there are action items that will take time to complete, add a date to each entry in the comments / notes section to see the timeline of the work underway.

Figure 18.2: Action Log Example

Annual Retreat Planning Committee – Action Log					
Action Item	**Most Responsible Person**	**Date Identified**	**Status**	**Date Completed**	**Comments/ Notes**
Finalize the contract for the venue space.	Albert	April 8	Complete	May 15	*April 24*– Draft contract developed. *April 11* - Pricing proposal received from venue.
Circulate the draft guest list to the team.	Sasha	April 16	Complete	April 18	*April 16* – Need to add the finance team.
Select the food option for lunch.	Susan	May 18	In Progress		*May 20* – Lunch menus received from venue.
Contact and confirm the keynote speaker.	Barb	May 18	Not Started		

Who is responsible for creating these documents?

Meeting minutes and action logs are the *responsibility of the meeting lead*, but can be delegated to someone else in attendance. If the note-taker or scribe role was taken on by another participant, consider asking them to manage the development of the meeting minutes or the ongoing tracking of the action log. Base this decision on the *complexity* of the discussion, and the *level of previous knowledge needed* to make sure the meeting minutes accurately reflect the conversation.

There are times when the *context* of the discussion is lost in the meeting minutes due to unfamiliarity with the *content*. If someone else is developing the meeting minutes or action log on your behalf, review these documents for accuracy after they are developed.

After these documents are drafted, *read them out loud* to make sure there is a good flow to the content, and consistency in your formatting.

What should be done with meeting minutes and action logs?

Place these documents in a *central location, such as a shared file share*, where they can be easily accessed later. The ability to refer to these documents is valuable. The location should be accessible and well-organized for easy retrieval.

When you develop your follow-up meeting email, plan to include these documents. This will be explored further in *Chapter 19: Develop and Circulate a Follow-Up Meeting Communication and Package*.

Step 1	Step 2	Step 3
Before	*During*	*After*

Develop and Circulate a Follow-Up Meeting Communication and Package

A lack of follow up is consistently expressed as a frustration by both meeting leads and participants. Considering the amount of effort it took to plan and lead a meeting, *don't let all the great work you completed fail to cross the finish line*. Reach out to your participants by developing and circulating a follow-up communication, along with any relevant documents that were reviewed or discussed.

This chapter will walk you through the importance of this post-meeting activity, what to include, who to send this to, and when this should be completed.

What is a follow-up meeting communication and package?

A follow-up meeting communication and package is *an important post-meeting activity that provides a summary of the key messages, results and appropriate documents to all individuals and groups invited.* This valuable source of information provides a high-level overview of the meeting and includes any meeting minutes, action logs, documents, and presentations that were viewed or discussed during the meeting.

This communication is typically *sent by, or on behalf of, the meeting lead.* Follow up is done by email, as this allows you to keep an electronic, time-stamped record of when the information was circulated, and to whom.

Why is it important to send a follow-up meeting communication and package?

When you closed out the meeting, you summarized the key points of the discussion. A follow-up communication *reiterates this information* and *sets strong, clear expectations* around the accountabilities of your participants.

By circulating a follow-up meeting communication and package, you will have *taken all reasonable steps* to actively communicate the meeting results. This demonstrates you intend to hold everyone accountable for their follow up responsibilities.

If you invited individuals that were unable to attend, a follow-up communication adds significant value by informing this group of the outcomes and next steps. This allows you to *avoid losing momentum*. Use this as a *great starting point to reach out* to see if they have any questions or feedback.

While it may feel like you are duplicating messages that were already provided at the end of your meeting, *don't skip over this important activity*. Post-meeting communication is essential as most business environments are extremely busy, and your participants have a variety of competing priorities. By reminding them of what they need to follow up on, you make sure their *action items are not lost in the shuffle* of their day-to-day work.

What should be included in a follow-up meeting communication and package?

When developing a follow-up communication, there are several key elements that should always be present. These include:

An introduction to the follow-up
The first line of your email should identify *what meeting you are referring to*, and remind them of the meeting purpose.

A summary of the discussion
Include a *high-level summary* of the meeting discussion, in no more than a few sentences. The remaining details of the discussion are included within your meeting minutes or action log.

Any decisions made

List any *decisions made* during the discussion. If it adds value, state the decision-making style used (directive, consultative, majority voting or consensus-based).

A list of action items and who is responsible

List what action items were identified, and who is responsible for each item. If these are embedded within the meeting minutes, *pull the action items into one consolidated list* that can be viewed in a glance.

A list of attached documents

List the documents you are attaching, such as the meeting minutes, presentations, and any other documents that were discussed or developed during the meeting.

Reiterate any post-meeting expectations

Once again, let the group know if there are any *expectations* such as sharing the information, keeping it confidential, following up on action items by a specific timeframe, etc.

The identified next steps

The last sentence or two should *summarize any next steps*.

The closing

As with any email, *close out the communication* with a farewell greeting of your choice, your name, and contact information.

What else should be considered when circulating a follow-up meeting communication and package?

The subject line

The subject line should clearly highlight that this is a follow-up email and indicate the specific meeting referenced. Consider starting your subject line with the words "Follow Up" to provide context before the reader opens the email.

Here are some examples of clear, post-meeting email subject lines:

• Follow Up: New Product Design Review Meeting
• Follow Up: Strategic Planning SWOT Analysis Meeting
• Follow Up: Summer Social Steering Committee Meeting
• FOLLOW UP: Centralized Scheduling Pilot Project Kick-Off Meeting
• FOLLOW UP: Financial Software RFP Evaluation Review Meeting

Who should the follow-up meeting communications and package be sent to?

When sending out a follow-up communication, consider including the groups outlined below. Use your *judgment, and unique meeting situation,* to determine who might be appropriate.

• All the invited participants who attended
• All the invited participants who were unable to attend
• Executive or administrative assistants to any participants
• Leaders and managers who are sponsors or champions of any projects or initiatives discussed at the meeting
• Anyone else who should be kept in the loop regarding the meeting's outcomes

When should a follow-up meeting communication and package be sent out?

When developing your follow-up communication, this should be done shortly after the meeting. The sooner your participants have this information, the better, as this *serves as a reminder for them to follow up on their action items*. This also allows them to *share any relevant information* with others.

Try to avoid extending this activity beyond two days after the meeting. The exception is when the meeting falls on the end of day Thursday or on a Friday, assuming weekends are not standard operating hours. In this case, the following Monday or early Tuesday is acceptable.

Examples of a follow-up meeting communication and package are included on the following pages.

Figure 19.1: Follow-Up Email Communication Example #1

Subject: FOLLOW UP: Financial Software RFP Evaluation Review Meeting - CONFIDENTIAL
Details: Good afternoon everyone, In follow up to this morning's meeting, here is a summary, and a list of action items for the group. We met today to *review the completed evaluations after the vendor demonstrations.* We collected some feedback on the evaluation process and reviewed the results of the scoring tool. The results brought back a clear, front-runner out of the three vendors. There was a **decision by consensus** that the preferred vendor would be taken forward as a recommendation to the steering committee. Our **action items** include: • *Prisha* will organize the next steering committee meeting and bring the recommendation forward, by next week. • *Jean* will contact the purchasing and legal departments to let them know we will be starting the contract negotiations shortly. • *Susanna* will submit the request for the funds to be spent in this fiscal year, at the next Financial Operations Committee meeting. The meeting minutes are attached. **Please keep this information confidential at this time.** We will reach out to you once the final decision has been reached by the steering committee. Watch your email for further updates. Thanks everyone for your ongoing support of this work.

This example references the meeting earlier this morning and offers a high-level summary of the discussion. This includes a decision made collectively by the group. The action items are listed, along with the attached document. Clear expectations are set that the meeting information should not be shared. Finally, the next steps are identified.

Figure 19.2: Follow-Up Email Communication Example #2

Subject: Follow Up: Centralized Scheduling Pilot Project Kick-Off Meeting

---

Details:

Good morning everyone,

In follow up to our *pilot project kick-off meeting* we held on Friday, here is a summary of the discussion, along with the decisions, action items, and next steps.

We began exploring the opportunity to **pilot a centralized model to scheduling**, to see if we can improve our processes, increase efficiencies, and improve the customer experience. After brainstorming the work involved, we have a better sense of what is needed to move this forward. We made the **decision to meet weekly** for the next three months.

The **action items** captured include:
- *Joel* will pull all the brainstormed activities into a document for the next meeting.
- *Stella* will bring preliminary data to the next meeting including the # of calls by department, new customer appointments, and average call time.
- *Adam* from the process improvement team will be added to the next meeting to begin discussing workflow.

A new action log has been started to track our action items and is attached. Watch your email for Friday meeting's agenda.

This second example references the kick-off meeting and provides a high-level summary. The decision by the team to meet weekly is highlighted. Action items are listed, with the most responsible person identified. The attachment is outlined, and the email ends with the next steps and expectations to watch for an agenda.

These examples demonstrate the information you should include. Use this activity to reiterate your expectations, and hold everyone accountable for their actions.

Chapter 20

Step 1
Before

Step 2
During

Step 3
After

Evaluate the Meeting and Capture Lessons Learned

By now, you planned, led and followed up on your meeting. As you start to wrap up the final activities in *The 3 Step Meeting Framework*™, reflect on, and evaluate the success of your meeting. First, take a step back and explore *if your expected outcomes became your actual outcomes*. Next, evaluate the meeting from a process perspective, and *identify opportunities for future improvements*. Capture any lessons learned and plan to apply these going forward.

This chapter explores how to evaluate your meeting to determine if it was successful, and what to do with these lessons learned.

Evaluate the expected outcomes

In the early stages of your meeting planning, you developed clear objectives and expected outcomes. Use these as a *baseline for comparison* to measure your success.

Your identified meeting objectives were *specific and measurable statements* that stated your goals for the meeting. The expected outcomes you developed were *the end results* you hoped to see. The meeting planning that followed should have set you on the path to accomplishing these goals and results.

Return to your developed objectives and expected outcomes from **Step 1: Before the Meeting**, and ask yourself the following questions:

• What were the **tangible and intangible results** from the meeting?
• Did the meeting discussion **focus on the identified objectives**?
• Did you **achieve** all the expected outcomes?
• Was anything **missed** during the discussion?
• Is any **follow up needed** that was not previously identified during the meeting?

If you successfully achieved your expected outcomes, *you did a great job of planning and leading the meeting* to make this happen. Use this learning to apply the same principles again, the next time. Despite any challenges that came up or circumstances that were out of your control, you managed them well and focused on achieving what you set out to do.

If you didn't achieve all your outcomes, consider this as *a great learning opportunity*. Think about what you can take away from this experience. Determine what you could do differently next time to prevent the same challenge from occurring. Did you have too many objectives? Did you need more time?

Going back to the examples discussed earlier in in *Chapter 4: Determine Your Meeting Objectives and Expected Outcomes*, here are a few examples of how you can evaluate your meeting:

---

*Meeting #1: You have identified the need to hold an **education** meeting.*

In this example, you were bringing all the staff together to complete a mandatory, one-hour health and safety training session. You identified your objectives as:

• Increase the awareness and understanding of the health and safety policies and procedures.
• Achieve a passing grade on the five-question quiz at the end of the session by all staff.
• Confirm that 100% of staff attend and complete this mandatory training by the end of the quarter.

Ask yourself what the results were from this meeting. Are the staff more aware, and have a greater understanding of the policies and procedures? While this is qualitative in nature, you can certainly say yes, if they were all present and engaged. Did they all pass the final quiz and answer at least 3 out of 5 questions correctly? This is quantitative, and you can definitively identify if yes, they all passed, or no, they did not. Finally, by capturing attendance, you can identify if 100% of staff attended this session.

Meeting #2: You have identified the need to hold an ***information sharing*** *meeting.*

In this example, you were kicking off a new initiative and wanted to bring everyone impacted by this work together to share the details known to date. You identified the objectives as:

- Achieve a shared understanding of the new initiative including the current challenges, goals, scope, target timeline, and baseline data.
- Determine who should participate on the project team to support the initiative.

When evaluating this meeting, ask yourself if everyone now has a shared understanding of the new initiative. Also, did you walk away with a list of names to include as part of the project team? If you can answer yes to both, then you were successful in achieving your objectives and expected outcomes.

Evaluate the meeting process

You can also evaluate the meeting from a process perspective. This includes *identifying any improvements for future meetings*. Evaluate everything about your meeting, from start to finish.

Take all the activities into consideration and ask yourself *what you feel you did well, what didn't work so well, and what you would do differently next time.* Since every meeting is unique, there are always opportunities to take key lessons from each of these experiences. Although the steps and activities of ***The 3 Step Meeting Framework*™** do not change, evaluating how you implemented them can always be a great source of learning.

Here are several, sample questions to ask yourself when evaluating your meeting from a *process point of view*:

• Did you send out the agenda and any documents far enough in advance to allow time for review?
• Did you provide enough time before the meeting for set up? Were there any unexpected challenges?
• Did you have the right people at the table? Did anyone unexpectedly not show up?
• Were your participants actively engaged in the discussion?
• Did the discussion stay on track? If not, were you able to navigate it back to the intended agenda topic?
• Did any technology glitches occur? Were there any audiovisual equipment issues?
• Were there any challenging discussions? Were they managed well?
• Did the room layout work for the needs of your meeting?
• Did you remember to invite the group to provide feedback at the end of the meeting?

These sample questions are meant to get you thinking about what you did well, and where improvements could be made. Remember also to *review any information you collected at the evaluation check-in*, near the end of the meeting. In the spirit of continuous improvement, identify at least one thing you could do better for the next meeting. Even with years of meeting management experience, there are always *opportunities for fine-tuning*.

Determine what lessons you personally learned from each meeting and keep track of these over time. By documenting this learning for your own use, you start to create your *own, valuable source of lessons learned to apply to future meeting planning*. As you go forward, revisit this periodically to leverage your previous learning.

How else can feedback be collected to evaluate the meeting?

You collected input from your participants at the end of the meeting discussion and self-evaluated the meeting from an outcome and process perspective. If you feel that *further feedback would be valuable*, there are additional ways to solicit input from the group. This can be through an *email request* for additional feedback, or an *online survey* that is circulated to the participants.

When sending an email request for feedback, *be specific in your ask* for more input. Determine what you want their feedback about, and keep your questions focused.

Post-meeting surveys are another way to capture more detailed information and can be anonymous if needed. Save these for times when additional feedback is essential. Completing surveys take time away from other tasks, and survey fatigue can result if too many are circulated.

If you do opt to send out a survey, there are free tools available online, such as *Survey Monkey*. This and other tools allow you to pull together a quick questionnaire that is sent out to collect feedback.

Take the time to examine how effective and successful your meeting was by determining if you accomplished what you set out to do. In addition, gain some valuable insight on how you implemented the steps and activities in the meeting process, to allow you to keep improving.

Apply your lessons learned going forward to all future meetings. This will allow you to continue to lead more effective meetings, especially as you become more familiar with *The 3 Step Meeting Framework™*. As you improve your meeting management skills, you will begin to consistently achieve the results you want, greater collaboration will take place, and all your projects and initiatives will move forward successfully.

| Step 1 *Before* | Step 2 *During* | Step 3 *After* |

Follow Up on Any Outstanding Action Items

After you have successfully planned, lead and followed up on your meeting, *check once again to see if there are any outstanding actions items.* Follow up can be done by reaching out to your participants, or by adding it as an agenda item at a future meeting.

This chapter briefly outlines why it's important to follow up on any outstanding action items, how to do this activity, and what to do if your participants fail to follow through on their responsibilities.

Why is it important to follow up on outstanding action items?

Action items captured during your meeting outlined what follow-up tasks or activities were needed, and who was required to do them. This activity is important as it holds everyone accountable for what they agreed to do. Action items *must be completed to keep projects and initiatives moving.*

How should follow up be done for outstanding action items?

Periodically, check your follow-up communication, meeting minutes, or action log, and close out any action items that are complete. Outstanding items can be followed up on by reaching out directly to the identified owner, or by placing them on a future agenda for a status update. How this activity occurs can be managed based on whether the meeting was a one-time only meeting or part of a series of ongoing meetings.

Following up after a one-time-only meeting
If you don't require another meeting, *follow up with the action item owner* by email again, or by phone. When reaching out, identify that you are following up to get a status update on the specific action item. Let them know you are continuing to track these to make sure they are completed.

Following up for ongoing meetings
Add the expectation of a *status update* by *placing it on a future meeting agenda,* if you are holding ongoing meetings. Review the list of identified action items at your next meeting with all your participants, and ask for updates. If you are keeping an action log, add the progress updates directly into the document.

What should be done if participants fail to follow up on action items?

The goal is to *hold everyone accountable* and to keep this work documented. If any of your participants are having trouble completing them, ask them what you can do to support them to allow them to be successful.

If you still find that certain participants are unresponsive after several attempts to hold them accountable, identify who would be appropriate to *escalate* this to, if needed. Add others to the communication such as appropriate leaders, champions, and sponsors. If you still have no response after multiple attempts, identify the direct leader of that participant, and reach out to request their assistance.

Step 1	Step 2	Step 3
Before	*During*	*After*

Plan Any Follow-Up Meetings and Apply Lessons Learned

The meeting is now officially over. You planned all the details in **Step 1: Before the Meeting**, lead the discussion in **Step 2: During the Meeting**, and followed up, and held everyone accountable in **Step 3: After the Meeting**. By now, you should have successfully walked through each of the steps and activities of *The 3 Step Meeting Framework™*, and seen positive results.

You *learned the methodology, assessed your own gaps* and *implemented the steps and activities* in your own meeting. Next, apply this approach and learning as you go forward to plan any follow-up or future meetings that arise. As you continue to build on this learning and consistently apply *The 3 Step Meeting Framework™*, you will eventually *reach a level of meeting mastery* that few have the know-how to achieve.

Plan any follow-up or other future meetings

If one of your identified action items is to book a follow-up meeting, continue to use *The 3 Step Meeting Framework™* to easily guide you through the steps again. Even if follow-up meetings are not required, you will still have many other meetings that arise.

Apply your lessons learned

You had two important opportunities to pause and evaluate your meeting. The first was when you closed out your meeting. The second was when you reflected on the meeting, from start to finish. Now, you have a *wealth of useful knowledge to apply to your future meetings*. Because each meeting is unique, new learning will always take place and accumulate. Take that cumulative knowledge and apply these valuable lessons as you go forward.

While the steps and activities are standardized and will never change, there are still various details of your meeting that are situation-specific. Continue to apply your new-found knowledge in all your future meetings.

Chapter 23

Conclusion to *The 3 Step Meeting Framework*™

Well, it has been quite a journey. I'm sure you can agree that *there are more to meetings than most people or organizations realize*. And since they make up a lot of what we do every day, it shouldn't come as a surprise. Every meeting is unique with different meeting purposes, objectives and expected outcomes, participants, agendas, etc.

This book has walked you *the three steps in the framework* and gave you a number of things to consider *before, during, and after* a meeting. This consisted of *25 standardized activities* to follow, each and every time you hold a meeting. No matter how unique your meeting is, the same steps and activities will continue to apply. This is the concept I introduced you to at the beginning around *appropriate standardization*.

Let's review the steps and activities once again.

Step 1: BEFORE the Meeting

1.	Define the **meeting purpose**.
2.	Determine the **meeting objectives and expected outcomes**.
3.	Identify the **right people** to invite.
4.	Determine the **right format** for your meeting.
5.	Identify the **meeting logistics**.
6.	Develop and circulate a **meeting appointment**.
7.	Create a clear, sequenced **agenda**.
8.	Determine the **room layout** for your meeting.
9.	Determine the **resources and tools** you need.
10.	Develop and circulate a **meeting communication and package**.

Step 2: DURING the Meeting

1.	**Set up** before the meeting.
2.	**Welcome** the participants and **capture attendance**.

3.	**Review the agenda** and **lay out expectations**.
4.	Provide **high-level context-setting** including the purpose, objectives and expected outcomes.
5.	**Lead** the meeting discussion.
6.	**Capture and document** the meeting discussion.
7.	Review the **action items** and define the **next steps**.
8.	Set any **post-meeting expectations**.
9.	**Evaluate** the meeting and **capture any lessons learned**.
10.	**Thank** your participants and **close** the meeting.

Step 3: AFTER the Meeting

1.	Collect all **meeting notes** and develop **meeting minutes or an action log**.
2.	Develop and circulate a **follow-up meeting communication and package**.
3.	**Evaluate** the meeting outcomes and process.
4.	Follow up on all **action items**.
5.	Plan any required **follow-up meetings** and apply **lessons learned** to future meetings.

As a senior project management consultant, I typically spend anywhere from four to six hours in meetings every day. The lessons and considerations you read throughout this book have come directly from years of *trial and error* while leading and participating in meetings. I have *taken these lessons learned and distilled them into an easy, straightforward methodology*. This proven approach has been time-tested, over and over again, with excellent results.

As I stated at the beginning, each of you are *coming from a different perspective*. What you take away from this experience will be different, as well. What I want you to do is to think about what you are already doing well, and where there are opportunities to make improvements. Apply these simple, standardized steps and activities, and *begin to see results immediately*.

I continue to experience great success thanks to my ability to lead effective meetings, and to facilitate the forward movement of many significant initiatives and projects. *Meetings are a powerful enabler to allow you to achieve success in your career.* I want you to experience the same success. Let me share this with you.

In fact, share your experiences and successes with me. *I would love to hear from you.* Tell me what worked well, what didn't work so well, and what you will do differently. The learning should continue. I still learn new lessons every day. You may have noticed, on the cover, this is the 1st edition. Don't be surprised if new lessons show up in future editions of this book.

If you enjoyed this book and found the information helpful, please *place a review where you made your purchase.* Share your experience with others. This would be kindly appreciated. The sooner we get this valuable information out there, the sooner that meetings don't have to be a source of anxiety, boredom and stress any longer.

Thank you for selecting **Unleash Your Meeting Potential**™: *A Comprehensive Guide to Leading Effective Meetings.*

Sincerely,
Natalie Berkiw, PMP

Chapter 24

Additional Resources

Watch for this book **Unleash Your Meeting Potential™** in the following formats:

• Hardcover
• Paperback
• eBook
• Audiobook

1. Follow along and apply your learning with exercises, templates, and examples in the **Unleash Your Meeting Potential™ Workbook**.

2. Keep a visual reminder of *The 3 Step Meeting Framework™* in your office, cubicle, lunchroom, boardroom, and more with the **Unleash Your Meeting Potential™ 16"x 20" Wall Poster** (*see next page for sample*).

3. Take advantage of available tools and templates for all your meeting communications in the **Unleash Your Meeting Potential™ Template Toolkit**.

4. Read the latest meeting tips, articles, and **blog posts** on the website: **www.EffectiveMeetings101.com** website. Sign up here for our email newsletter.

5. Watch for the upcoming **Unleash Your Meeting Potential™ Online Course**. Details will be posted on the website, when available.

6. Connect directly for **personal coaching and support** to implement *The 3 Step Meeting Framework™* in your organization.

Figure 24.1: Unleash Your Meeting Potential™ 16" x 20" Wall Poster

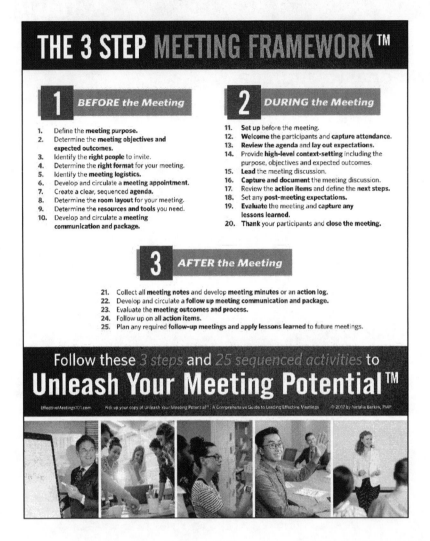

Order your copy of the above, full color **Unleash Your Meeting Potential™ 16" x 20" Wall Poster** at **www.EffectiveMeetings101.com**.

Printed on high quality, 100 lb gloss poster paper.

To learn more or to order any of the above additional resources, please visit **www.EffectiveMeetings101.com**, or contact the author directly:

Natalie Berkiw, PMP
natalieberkiw@gmail.com

Chapter 25

Acknowledgements

A special thank you to my editor, Brenda (pro_writer100), for the attention and care in making sure this book was polished and complete.

I would like to acknowledge the beautiful cover design by Kir@n99 from 99designs, who took my vision and turned it into reality.

Thank you to the following photographers/artists who are featured throughout this book:

- Dashu83
- Freepik
- Jannoon028
- Javi_indy
- Katemangostar
- Kues1
- Nensuria
- Onlyyouqj
- Peoplecreations
- Pressfoto
- Topntp26

Personal Notes and Learning:

Personal Notes and Learning:

Personal Notes and Learning:

Personal Notes and Learning:

Made in the USA
Las Vegas, NV
22 January 2024

84746441R00116